Victor Bethell

Ten Days At Monte Carlo At The Bank's Expense

Containing Hints to Visitors and a General Guide to the Neighbourhood

Victor Bethell

Ten Days At Monte Carlo At The Bank's Expense
Containing Hints to Visitors and a General Guide to the Neighbourhood

ISBN/EAN: 9783337125493

Printed in Europe, USA, Canada, Australia, Japan

Cover: Foto ©Andreas Hilbeck / pixelio.de

More available books at **www.hansebooks.com**

Ten Days
At Monte Carlo

At the Bank's Expense

Containing

Hints to Visitors

and

A General Guide to the Neighbourhood

By V. B.

With a Map

London
William Heinemann
1898

TO MY FRIEND

W. B.

I DEDICATE THESE PAGES

IN GRATEFUL REMEMBRANCE OF MUCH KINDNESS AND

HOSPITALITY RECEIVED AT HIS HANDS.

V. B.

INTRODUCTION

Ask any one who has visited Monte Carlo how they like the place, the majority will say: "Oh, it's all very well for a day or two, but there's nothing on earth to be done there, except the gambling, and as nobody ever wins, it becomes very expensive after a time!"

I once knew a honeymoon couple, who spent a month there. I dined with them the night before they left, and found they were utterly sick of it, and vowed they would never come again; and when I learnt how they had spent their time, I was not surprised.

Their programme was as follows:—they got up late, took a stroll for about half-an-hour on the Terrace, and then went and lunched heavily at Ciro's. This took from twelve till two, after which they went straight over to the gambling-rooms, and played steadily till 6.30. They then went home and dressed, and had a long and rich dinner either at the Paris or the Grand,

Introduction

after which they again repaired to the Rooms and gambled until closing-time. At the end of a month, I found they had never taken a walk or even a drive; they had never been to Cap Martin or La Turbie, and did not even know that one of the loveliest orchestras in Europe could be heard almost every day free of charge. Eating, drinking, and gambling had been their daily programme, and of course they departed feeling very ill, and much annoyed with themselves for having lost a considerable sum of money.

This was an exaggerated case, no doubt, but I have met hundreds nearly as bad, and it is for the enlightenment of such as these that I take up my feeble pen. We are not *all* ardent cyclists, I am aware, although it is daily becoming more rare to find any one under fifty who does not 'bike': still, as a general rule, wherever a bicycle can go a carriage can follow, and if I succeed in persuading only a few to leave the unhealthy atmosphere of the Casino on a fine day and explore the beauties of this lovely country—whether it be on a 'bike,' in a carriage, or on foot—I shall consider that my labours have not been in vain. It may be as well to mention that none of the rides, herein described, are beyond the powers of even the average lady cyclist.

Introduction

As regards the Roulette, please let it be understood that I do not for a moment profess to have discovered an infallible system. It has been my principal study to discover why most people lose, and having more or less arrived at that, I have endeavoured to frame a system on entirely opposite lines. Personally, I never could see the fun of losing money at the tables. You see some people going in day after day, never coming out with a fifty-centime piece, and yet thoroughly enjoying themselves. To my mind this is incomprehensible. It is not so much the loss of the money, as the sense of defeat, which annoys me, and if the Bank worsted me two days in succession, I should probably relinquish the struggle. I would rather sit for hours to win a five-franc piece than come out a loser.

I quite recognize the fact that my system is of no use to gamblers; they would rather lose their money than attempt to play it; but should there be a few people, who are obliged to remain at Monte Carlo for several months, and whom it might amuse to win a louis or two a day, I recommend them to try it.

The numbers given herein, actually did turn up at the table mentioned, on ten consecutive days. There can be no fairer test for any system, and I honestly believe, that if a thousand people were to come down, armed with sufficient capital,

Introduction

and were to play the system to win £50 a day each, the Administration of the Casino would very soon be compelled to close their doors.

THE AUTHOR.

Monte Carlo,
  May 15, 1898.

CONTENTS

CHAPTER I
Frank Curzon talks of Monte Carlo, and Wilfrid Blundell—The Game of Roulette—Percentages in favour of the Bank—Why most people lose—The American System-Players and their System . 1

CHAPTER II
Blundell and his System—Frank Curzon and I decide to give it a trial 12

CHAPTER III
Preparations for Monte Carlo — Bicycles on the Riviera—The Touring Club de France—Smith's Bank—Casino Customs—'The Viatique'—Press Subsidies—Blackmailers defeated . . . 26

CHAPTER IV
Hints for the Journey—The Train de Luxe—The Yankee and his distinguished Card-sharper—Climate of Monte Carlo—Ciro and Ciro's Restaurant—Lunch at Ciro's—First Day's Play . 37

CHAPTER V
First Bicycle Ride—La Crémaillère—La Turbie—Corniche Road—Valley of the Paillon—Eze—Cap Martin—Lunch at Cap Martin Hotel—Second Day's Play 53

CHAPTER VI
Second Bicycle Ride—Monte Carlo to Nice—The Legend of Saint Dévote—Beaulieu—Villefranche—The 'London House'—Third Day's Play—Concert at the Casino—The Monte Carlo Orchestra 65

Contents

CHAPTER VII

Third Ride—La Turbie—The Monastery of Laghet—'Ex Votos'—The Gold-embroidered Slippers of the Comtesse de R——.—Laghet to Nice—St. Jean—Cap St. Hospice—Fourth Day's Play—A Triumph for the System 78

CHAPTER VIII

Fourth Ride—Railway of the Sud de la France—Nice—Colomars—Tourettes—Vence—Cagnes—Fifth Day's Play—French 'as she is spoke' at the Tables—Restaurant of the Hôtel de Paris—Monsieur Fleury 93

CHAPTER IX

Fifth Ride—Grasse—Fragonard and his famous Panels—Magagnosc—Villeneuve-Loubet—Sixth Day's Play 105

CHAPTER X

Sixth Ride—Peillon—Peille—Pic de Baudon—Seventh Day's Play—Restaurant of the Grand Hotel—François 119

CHAPTER XI

Seventh Ride—The Man who played successfully for Ten Years—Cagnes—Biot—Antibes—Juan-les-Pins—Cap d'Antibes—Eighth Day's Play—Hôtel Terminus at Nice 134

CHAPTER XII

Eighth Ride—Puget-Théniers—Entrevaux—Touet de Beuil—La Mescla—St. Martin du Var—Ninth Day's Play 144

CHAPTER XIII

Ninth Ride—Laghet—Contes—Nice-Riquier—Tenth Day's Play—Summary of Ten Days' Results—Total Expenses and Net Profit . . 154

CHAPTER XIV

The Hotels and Restaurants of Monte Carlo—Monte Carlo Sharps and Swindlers—Hints to Visitors . 162

Addenda 179

THE RESTAURANT AND HOTEL L'HERMITAGE
MONTE CARLO.

AFFILIATED WITH THE PRINCES' RESTAURANT, LONDON.

The most luxurious and best appointed Establishment in Monte Carlo, with full South View of the Mediterranean.

A special advantage to Visitors is afforded by the Spacious Gardens attached to the Premises, and its close proximity to the Casino.

Acting Directors:
V. BENOIST and G. FOURAULT.

The Princes' Restaurant
PICCADILLY, LONDON, W.

Universally admitted to be the most fashionable Rendezvous in London

FOR

LUNCHEONS, DINNERS AND SUPPERS.

BOCCHI'S ORCHESTRA.

Managing Director: GUSTAVE FOURAULT.

(a)

The Man of the World

A HIGH-CLASS WEEKLY NEWSPAPER

PUBLISHED EVERY WEDNESDAY

PRICE TWOPENCE

THE MAN OF THE WORLD GOES ALL OVER THE WORLD

OFFICES—
52 Fleet Street, LONDON, E.C.

READ

"The Rialto"

The Best City Weekly

TEN DAYS AT MONTE CARLO

CHAPTER I

Frank Curzon talks of Monte Carlo, and Wilfrid Blundell—The Game of Roulette—Percentages in favour of the Bank—Why most people lose—The American System-Players and their System.

FRANK CURZON and I had always been chums. We had been at the same house at Eton together, and had gone up to New College, Oxford, at about the same time. After that he went to the Bar, and I went into the City, so we rather lost sight of one another, except for casual meetings at the Club.

One evening last November I found him dining alone at the Club, so went and sat at the same table. We began with the usual abuse of the weather, which had been rather excelling itself, even for November in London. Morning after morning we had awoke, with a sort of choking sensation in our throats, and had sat down to breakfast by lamp-light: this sort of thing was usually accompanied by a raw easterly wind, which if it did succeed in somewhat dispelling the fog, generally brought rain in the course of the day. London was certainly most gloomy and depressing.

"Thank goodness," said Frank, "I shall hope to see the sun again in about a fortnight's time; I am off for my annual trip to Monte Carlo."

"The Bar must be looking up, old chap," said I, "if it will run to annual trips to Monte Carlo; I suppose it will cost you a couple of hundred at least, and the City won't stand that, with business as it is at present."

"I've no doubt," he replied, "that it costs most people all that, and *some* people a great deal more, but I shall be very much surprised if it costs *me* anything at all; at any rate it hasn't done so for the last five years."

"What is the secret?" I inquired.

"Simply this," he said; "you have no doubt heard the old story that 'Rouge perd, et noir perd, mais c'est toujours Blanc, qui gagne'; in my case I can only say that 'Rouge perd quelquefois, et noir perd quelquefois, mais Blanc perd toujours,' and as long as Monsieur Blanc, or rather the long-suffering shareholders of the Monte Carlo Casino, continue to pay my expenses, as they have always done up to the present, so long shall I continue to spend my Christmas amongst them."

"Do you mean to tell me, then, that you have discovered an infallible system?"

"No," said Frank, "I won't go quite so far as to say that, because, with all due respect to the Vatican, I don't believe that anything in this world is infallible; but what I do believe is, that as long as I continue to play on the same system, as I have done for the last five years, it is good to bet odds on my defeating the Bank; and as I hold an unbeaten certificate up to the present, it is difficult to say what those odds really are."

"Is the system your own invention," I inquired, "or were you shown it by some one?"

"I got the idea," he said, "from a very shrewd person whom I came across during my first visit to the place. I was given a letter of introduction to a man called Wilfred Blundell. He has lived at Monte Carlo for a good number of years, but is not allowed to gamble, as he holds an official position there; he may consequently be regarded as the looker-on who sees most of the game.

"I had several long talks with Blundell, and

found that he had many interesting theories regarding gamblers, and the Bank.

"He was rather a reticent person, but if you got him all to yourself, especially after dinner, and started him on his favourite topic, you could learn a lot from him.

"Well, one evening, after an excellent dinner that I had given him at Ciro's, he asked me to come round to his rooms, and sample his cigars and old whisky.

"As soon as we were comfortably settled before a good fire, and had got our cigars and drinks well under way, I turned the conversation on to the subject of gambling, and found my host in an unusually communicative frame of mind.

"'You have no doubt often heard,' he said, 'and doubtless believe, that the Bank wins owing to the advantage which it has over the players. It is the popular belief that no system can succeed whilst the Bank possesses this advantage.

"'Now, in my opinion, the percentage in favour of the Bank is so small, that the serious system player need not even take it into consideration at all. It only affects people who play recklessly on numbers without realizing the folly of their game; but there are so many fools in the world, that in this respect the Bank does reap a very material benefit.

Ignorance of Players

"'It was only the other evening that I almost quarrelled with one of my oldest friends, through trying to convince her of this fact. Mrs. Henry Walsh has, to my certain knowledge, lost about £500 a year at Monte Carlo, regularly for the last twenty years, simply through playing recklessly on the numbers, and transversals, without any system at all. Although she is in other respects an intelligent and highly cultivated old lady, it is quite impossible to convince her of the folly of her ways, for she firmly believes that her losses are entirely due to her bad luck, and nothing else. She got quite angry when I told her that people who were content to play on even chances were just twice as likely to win, in the long run, as people who played on numbers; and when I told her that the more numbers you covered, the less likely you were to win, on a series of "coups," she told me "I was talking utter nonsense, and that, as *she* had played the game for twenty years, and *I* had never played at all, she must know more about it than I did!". So I have given her up as hopeless, and as long as she is well enough to come to Monte Carlo and gamble, so long can the shareholders of the Casino count upon a certain £500 a year.

"'Possibly you yourself have never realized the true percentage of advantage that the Bank has over the player. Most people will tell you that the Bank has one chance better than you in every thirty-seven spins. This is quite correct if you only play on one number "en plein," but if you play on an even chance the Bank has only half this advantage over you, or one chance better than you in every seventy-four spins, the reason being that when your stake is on an even chance, and zero appears, you do not lose your whole stake, but only half of it: the player always having the right to take off half his stake.

"'You would think, then, that it would be fairly obvious to most people, that if you put a louis on the first eighteen numbers "en plein," instead of putting eighteen louis on "manque," you are doing a very foolish thing; for when zero comes out, as it should do once in every thirty-seven spins, you would lose the whole of your eighteen louis, whereas if you had put them on to "manque," you only lose nine of them; in other words, the man who plays on the numbers is quite sure to lose, on the average, nine louis an hour more than the man who plays on "manque."

"'Yet you would be surprised to find how few of the people who come and play in these Rooms have grasped even this elementary fact. Much less have they grasped the fact, that the more numbers they cover, the less chance they have of winning.

The Bank's Percentage

"'It was only the other day that I was enunciating this theory to a man, who had been here very often, and won and lost thousands of pounds. He could not see it, so I said, "Not only is what I say a positive fact, but I can prove to you that if you cover sufficient numbers, the Bank has a 100 per cent. advantage over you!"

"'He said the idea of such a thing was quite absurd, and offered to bet me £10 that I was wrong. I took the bet, and proceeded to explain to him that if he staked one piece "en plein" on thirty-five numbers, he could lose thirty-five pieces if one or two numbers came out, and the most he could possibly win per "coup" was one piece: he was, therefore, laying 35 to 1, when the real odds were 35 to 2, or $17\frac{1}{2}$ to 1: he was, therefore, laying double the proper odds, or in other words, giving the Bank an advantage of 100 per cent. He was bound to admit that my demonstration was sound, and paid up the £10 on the spot.

"'Perhaps you are not aware, that if you back any given dozen, the Bank has a four per cent. advantage over you, and if you are foolish enough to back two dozens for the same spin, the Bank has an eight per cent. advantage over you. For if you back one dozen the Bank only bets you two to one that twenty-five numbers will beat twelve, whereas the proper odds are 2·08 to one. And, in the same way, if you back two dozens, the Bank makes *you* lay two to one that twenty-four numbers will beat thirteen, whereas the proper odds are only 1·84 to one, and you consequently have a disadvantage of eight per cent. in the odds.'

"I had now got Blundell fairly started on his favourite topic, and had only got to put in a question or two occasionally to keep him talking.

"'Then,' I said, 'your theory is that most gamblers are fools, and do not take the trouble to work out the different chances of the table?'

"'Yes,' said Blundell, 'I am sure that not one per cent. of the people playing in those Rooms at the present moment realize the facts that I have just explained to you, and you could probably win a bet of £10, in the same way that I did, every other day.

"'I can give you a very striking example of this,' he continued. 'About two years ago, the gambling establishments in New York were closed up by the police, and the men who kept the tables, and their croupiers, were consequently turned loose on society, without an occupation. Having nothing better to do, as long as New York continued in a moral frame of mind, a

The American System-Players

number of these men formed a syndicate, and came over to play at Monte Carlo, on a system.

"'They had a large capital at their back, and were content with small gains, and the result was that after a campaign of some four months, they went away small winners.

"'Knowing that they were professional gamblers, who were playing on a system to make money, and not merely as an amusement, I thought it would be interesting to find out what the system consisted in, and so made friends with one of them. He made a tremendous secret of the so-called system, and told me that the man who invented it had spent years and years in working it out, and that it was based on the study of some hundreds of thousands of spins of the Roulette. At last I got him to show it to me. It was most disappointing, very complicated, and based on a fallacy. Some cranky individual, who had been spinning a Roulette Wheel for years, thought he had discovered, that after a given number had appeared, certain numbers were more likely to come out than others. He had drawn up the most elaborate and complicated tables, giving the numbers to be staked on, after any given number had come out. They played on about eight numbers every spin of the wheel, and if luck went against them gradually increased their stakes.

"'The man appeared surprised when I pointed out to him that by playing on eight numbers every "coup," they gave the Bank an advantage of three per cent., whereas if they played on even chances, that advantage would only be 1·35 per cent. He said that their discovery was worth more than 1·65 per cent., and that the proof of this was that they were winning every day. I thought it was no good arguing the point, but I felt quite sure, in my own mind, that their so-called "discovery" amounted to nothing at all, and that they won simply because they were content to play systematically, to win very small stakes, with a large capital behind them.'

"'Then,' I observed, 'you think that you know of a system by which it is possible to do this with comparatively little risk?'

"'Yes,' he replied; 'I could have shown those professionals a system on even chances, by which they would have won from eighty to a hundred louis a day, with the same capital they possessed, and with far less risk than they were taking by playing on the numbers.'

"'Did you show it to them?' I asked.

"'No,' he answered, 'I never show it to any but intimate friends, and I should never advise any one to try it unless I knew that he possessed the necessary capital.'

"'How much capital is required?' I asked.

"'At least two hundred pounds to play it in louis,' said Blundell.

"'I have got more than that with me at present,' I said; 'do you mind showing it to *me?* and I will give it a trial.'

"'Certainly,' he replied, 'if you will come and lunch with me to-morrow, I will show it to you after lunch, and you can put it to the test.'

"'Very many thanks,' said I. 'Good-night!'"

CHAPTER II

Blundell and his System—Frank Curzon and I decide to give it a trial.

By this time Frank Curzon and I had finished dinner, and he proposed that if I was interested, and cared to hear all about Blundell and his system, we had better adjourn to his rooms, where he had all the figures of his play for the last five years, exactly as he had worked them at the tables.

We accordingly went round, and Frank proceeded to explain to me the system, as shown him by Blundell.

It appears that after many years of careful observation, Blundell had arrived at the following conclusions.

The reason why the Bank wins with such regularity, is not because it has a great advantage over the players in the percentage, but because it is a machine, with a practically unlimited capital, playing mechanically against a

Why the Bank Wins

host of players, most of whom possess no capital at all, and all of whom, at a critical moment, are liable to lose their tempers and their nerve.

The punter is also habitually greedy. What player do you know who is content to go into the Casino, and make even ten per cent. a day net profit on his capital?

Most of your gambling friends would laugh at the idea! They all expect to double their capital, and most of them hope to make four or five hundred per cent. And yet the Bank in a good year only makes about one per cent. a week, or fifty per cent. per annum! If the Bank expected to win in the same proportion as most of the players, its expectations would amount to the modest little sum of about four hundred millions sterling per annum!

The Bank certainly has a great advantage in the point of capital, it has the advantage of being a machine, and it also possesses the advantage of the limit, but against all this you must remember that the punter has also two great pulls in his favour. He can continue playing as long as he is a loser, and can run away the moment he is a winner; and he can vary his stake according to whether his luck is good or bad. To put it in vulgar parlance, "the Bank has to stand up to be shot at."

This being so, we must make as much use as

possible of our advantages, and endeavour to reduce those of the Bank to a minimum. In order to do this, we must fight them with their own weapons, so to speak, and attacking them with a large capital, be content to make a small percentage on our money.

We must play cautiously, and 'go very slow,' when luck is against us, and the moment the luck turns sufficiently to give us a small profit on the day, we must leave off at once and give the game a rest till the next day.

Ninety-nine per cent. of all the systems ever invented fail for want of sufficient capital; the remaining one per cent. are defeated by the maximum.

Therefore, the only way to hope for success, is to attack the Bank with a large capital, in such a way that the maximum will probably never be reached.

A very essential point about a good system is simplicity. The more elaborate and complicated your system may be, the more certain it is to fail. There is no doubt that the croupiers will be on the look-out for the moment when you begin to get into deep water, and then, by spinning quicker than usual, they will prevent your working out any elaborate calculation, to arrive at the amount to be staked. They will flurry and bustle you, and endeavour to make you lose your head and your temper, at the critical moment, and from what I have seen myself and from what players themselves have told me, it is very certain that they often succeed.

It is no use people attempting to play a system at Monte Carlo unless they are specially qualified to undertake it. A few of the indispensable qualities are, a clear head, unlimited faith in the system, dogged perseverance, the best of good tempers, and plenty of pluck. Any one who does not possess all of the above qualifications, in addition to a few others, had better leave systems alone; for to play a system impatiently, timidly, or with insufficient capital is quite the surest way to lose.

Another very important point in playing a system, is to give the Bank as little advantage over you as possible; it 'goes without saying,' therefore, that all serious systems should always be played on the *even chances*.

If your system possesses staying power and is backed up by the necessary capital, the best thing to do when 'zero' or the 'refait' occurs, is to take off half your stake and regard the 'coup' as a loss. The amounts taken off the table in this way, would be placed aside and added to your net profits at the end of the day. It will be shown, in due course, that this 'Zero

Sinking Fund' forms a nice little addition to the player's profits, and instead of 'zero' proving a thorn in your side, it will be seen that the oftener 'zero' appears during the play, the greater your net gains will be, provided you are able to bring the score level before leaving off.

This method of dealing with 'zero' is adopted by hardly any players, as far as I know, but seems to me by far the most sensible, and certainly the simplest plan, always provided that your system is strong enough to stand it.

Most systems fail because the stakes are increased too quickly: the player gets into big figures, strikes a run against himself, and is either defeated by the maximum, or from want of capital.

The fact of the matter is that he is too greedy, and has not sufficient patience. If he commences by losing, he is in too much of a hurry to get his money back. If he wins, at first, he stays on at the tables too long and exhausts his good luck, winning small sums, and when the bad luck sets in, he begins playing high stakes and losing.

Almost all systems are played with a progression, that is to say, increasing the stakes every 'coup' as long as you are a loser, and continuing to do so until losses are wiped out, and a profit appears.

Different Systems

Some people double their stakes after every losing 'coup,' playing 1, 2, 4, 8, 16, and so on, until they win a 'coup,' when they become the winner of one unit, whatever the unit in their game may be.

Others play 1, 3, 7, 15, etc., which means that they try to win a unit for every 'coup' played.

Needless to remark that both these systems are quite useless, for the moment the player strikes an adverse run of 11, he is defeated by the maximum, supposing him to have commenced with a stake of one louis, and such a run as this might be encountered almost every day.

A much better system is to play 1, 2, 3, 4, 5, etc. In other words, add one to your stake each time whether you lose or whether you win, and continue to do so until you have won at least one unit. This you count as one point gained, and start afresh to win another.

This is not at all a bad system, but cannot be played with safety with a unit of more than one louis, and even then requires a very large capital behind it.

The chief advantage in it is, that the player may win far less 'coups' than the Bank on the day, and yet come out a good winner at the finish.

The chief objection to it is, that in the event of continued bad luck, the stakes mount up too quickly; and I have seen 'tableaux' where the player would have been over two thousand louis out of pocket, and would have had to play one hundred and forty to one hundred and fifty louis at a stake in order to get back previous losses. The unit is also of necessity too small, and the player, consequently, has to remain too long at the tables in order to win anything appreciable.

My system is an improved edition of the above, and say we are provided with a capital of £600, can be played with a unit of five louis.

The amount we can win depends upon the number of hours we are prepared to remain at the tables, but for several reasons I don't think it would be wise to endeavour to win more than four units per day, or £16. Sometimes this can be done in five minutes, and sometimes it may take three hours, but on the average it should not take more than two hours per day.

Our unit of five louis will be found a very convenient one, because the Bank provides gold five-louis pieces, commonly known as 'plaques,' and this will make our calculations and stakes very simple.

Our game, then, is to win four of these 'plaques' every day, but we do not try to win them all at once, but one by one. As soon as we have succeeded in winning one unit we put it away in a separate pocket, rule off our score

The 'Avant Dernier'

and start afresh to win another. The winning of each and every 'plaque,' therefore, constitutes a distinct and separate operation.

The question now arises: What chance are we to play on, and how are we to vary our stakes? The first is not nearly so important as the second.

If the system is really good it ought not to matter much upon what it is played, provided always that it be an *even chance*. At the same time experience has taught me that by far the best chance adapted to our system is what is commonly known as the 'avant dernier.' This consists of always backing the colour that came out *last but one*.

For example, if on arriving at our table the colours had come up

R
B
R

our first stake would be on the Black, and then, no matter what turned up, our next stake would be on the Red.

In the same way if the table had run

R
R
B

our first stake would be on the Red, and our next on the Black.

By this means it will be seen that we get the advantage of all the long runs, on either colour, after the second 'coup,' and when the table runs intermittently Red, Black, Red, Black, we win every stake.

For example, if there is a run of eight, either on the Red or Black, we shall win six bets running in either case; and in the same way if the table runs Red, Black, Red, Black, eight times running, we shall win six consecutive bets.

The only two combinations that do not suit us are several runs of two and three in succession, for if the table runs

    R
    R
      B
      B
    R
    R
      B
      B

we shall lose every bet, and if it runs

    R
    R
    R
      B
      B
      B

the Bank wins two bets to our one.

The 'Avant Dernier'

However, taking everything into consideration, you will see very few records of the tables in which after, say a hundred 'coups,' by our method of staking, the player would not have won nearly as many bets as the Bank.

You will see records of a whole day's play, where Red has come up 50, 60, and even 70 times more than Black; but you will hardly ever see a record in which a player on the 'avant dernier' would have lost fifty 'coups' more than the Bank in the course of a day.

We will assume, then, that we have a capital of £600, and that we have decided to play on the 'avant dernier,' and to make our unit five louis; we have also decided to be content to win four units per day.

The best way to do this is to commence playing what are called 'flat stakes' of one unit (that is to say, we stake one unit every 'coup'), and continue doing so until either we are one to the good, or the Bank has won ten units from us.

The moment we are on the right side we slip the 'plaque' we have won into our waistcoat pocket, rule off our score on the score-sheet, and start afresh to try and win another one.

If, however, the Bank wins ten from us before we have won one from them, we then double our unit and continue playing flat stakes of two units until we have got back all our losses, when we once more go back to stakes of one unit.

In the event of the Bank still continuing to win, as soon as our score reaches − 30—*i. e.* as soon as the Bank has won ten stakes of two units more than ourselves—we then raise the unit to three 'plaques' (fifteen louis), and continue playing flat stakes of three until we have got all our losses back.

In the same way, should the ill luck still continue, we should raise the unit to four, when the score showed us to be − 60, and to five units when the score reached − 100.

By this means it will be seen that in the event of our having good luck at first, the *séance* is quickly over, and we retire from the contest with a win of twenty louis. But, should luck be against us at the start, we shall soon recoup our losses, when it comes over to our side, and in the event of several 'zeros' having appeared in the course of play, we may eventually only have to win one or two units, instead of the prescribed four.

If the *séance* be a short one, it will probably be found that we have won more bets than the Bank, but if we start by losing, and subsequently become winners, it will generally be found that the Bank has won more bets than ourselves.

For, supposing the Bank to start by getting ten bets ahead of us, we can get all our losses

Blundell's System

back by winning five; and if they get twenty bets ahead of us, it only takes us ten to recoup; and therein lies the strength of the system.

If we have good luck at first, we retire before it has time to change, and if we have bad luck at the start, by means of our system we are enabled to see it out, and get our losses back as soon as it changes.

I don't for a moment affirm that the system is infallible with a capital of £600! The more capital you have to fall back upon, the greater the certainty of success, but from what I have seen of the game, it seems to me to be very long odds on the player who has this amount of capital behind him.

This, then, was the system that Blundell had shown to Frank Curzon, and which the latter had found to be so entirely satisfactory.

Frank started by playing it in louis, to win five units per day, with a capital of £200, and after testing it for a week, he increased his capital to £300, and played it with a unit of two louis.

He now proposed that we should each put up £300, and that I should accompany him to Monte Carlo and play it with a unit of five louis.

He showed me all his figures for the last five years, comprising altogether about fifty days' play. It seems that in all his experience, he had only twice got into dangerous figures, and had to play with four times his unit.

On one of these occasions he had to remain at the tables for nearly 300 'coups,' and was at one moment as much as eight-four units out of pocket, but the luck then veered round, and he slowly got all his losses back. In this case he was not even obliged to continue until the score was quite square, as there was an amount of about ten units already standing to the credit of 'Zero Fund.'

It looked almost too good to be true, and if I had not known Frank to be perfectly reliable, I should hardly have believed his story.

It is a well-known fact that gamblers lie, like fishermen, but here in his figures, evidently worked at the tables, was unquestionable proof of all he had told me. One is so accustomed to hear it laid down that it is practically impossible to win at Monte Carlo, that one naturally doubts an assertion to the contrary, until one sees positive proofs.

When I came to Frank's rooms, the idea of accompanying him to Monte Carlo never entered my mind, now I had half a mind to go.

The fact of the matter was, that I had just come into a legacy of £500, and had determined to give it a chance in a West Australian mining gamble.

On Frank's showing, it was five to one on Monte Carlo turning up trumps, and if it did, I could still give Westralia a chance on my return.

"I'll think it over and let you know to-morrow," I said.

"All right," said Frank, as he opened the front door to let me out.

The weather was simply disgusting, it was raw and cold, a thick yellow fog had come on since dinner, and men were parading Piccadilly with torches.

"I don't think I need keep you waiting," I said, "the English climate has settled the question; I have decided to come and try my luck with you in the 'Sunny South.'"

"Right you are," said Frank, "we will discuss all our plans to-morrow."

CHAPTER III

Preparations for Monte Carlo—Bicycles on the Riviera—The Touring Club de France—Smith's Bank—Casino Customs—'The Viatique'—Press Subsidies—Blackmailers defeated.

"You must allow *me* to take command of this expedition," said Frank, when I met him next day by appointment, "and if you will permit me, I will proceed to give you an idea of our plan of campaign.

"We intend to combine business with pleasure, and the length of our business hours will depend entirely upon our good or bad fortune. With ordinary good luck you should not find them irksome. At the commencement they will doubtless be pleasurable and exciting, but the novelty will soon wear off, and then you will find our work becoming monotonous and tiresome.

"We must regard the gambling as serious business, for our pleasure will depend upon it.

The Touring Club de France

Outside 'the Rooms' we shall do our best to enjoy ourselves as much as possible.

"It is no use economizing on a pleasure trip, and any one wishing to travel 'on the cheap' had better give Monaco a very wide berth. You get the best of everything there, if you are prepared to pay for it cheerfully, but it is the last place in the world in which to worry about petty items of expenditure.

"We shall, therefore, take first return tickets, go down as luxuriously as possible, live like princes as long as the system works, and come back in the same style, if we defeat the Bank. If not, we must dispense with the 'luxe' on the return journey.

"We shall take down our 'bikes,' and I'll guarantee that you will know all the nice rides within easy reach of Monte Carlo before you return."

Frank then explained to me that he had written in course of the day to get me elected to the Touring Club de France, of which he is a member.

This is an institution to which every cyclist going abroad should belong. The subscription is only five shillings per annum, and it is well worth the money. They send you, gratis, a very pretty badge (which can be worn in your cap) and a card of Identification. On presenting these at any Custom-house on the French frontier, you are treated with the greatest courtesy, and are subjected to none of the annoyances to which an ordinary traveller with a cycle has to submit.

If you don't know a member to propose you, write to the President, 5 Rue Coq Héron, Paris, stating your full name, profession, and address, with your clubs (if any), and giving two references; send him a postal order for five shillings, and the chances are you will be elected within a fortnight.

The Club supplies, if required, at very moderate prices, road-books and maps for the whole of France, giving full particulars as to the routes, hotels, etc., and any one intending to 'bike' in the neighbourhood of Monte Carlo should provide himself with their publications for the departments of the Alpes Maritimes and The Var.

Another very excellent map is that of 'The Riviera' (Sud-Est), published by the Libraire Neal, 248 Rue Rivoli, Paris, and doubtless procurable in London, as it is priced on the cover in English money, one shilling and sixpence.

I have often been asked by friends, what is the best way to take a bicycle out to the Riviera, and what it costs. I can only say that it is just as easy for a member of the Touring Club to take a machine out to Monte Carlo, as it is to take one from London to Inverness, and it probably runs less risk on the way.

On no account bother about a crate of any sort or kind; they give a lot of trouble, and greatly increase the expense. The most I would advise you to do, is to have the pedals removed, have the parts liable to rust lightly smeared over with vaseline, and wrapped round with calico or flannel. Be careful to leave the wheels free to revolve, so that the machine can be wheeled about in the ordinary way.

You will find the railway employés more considerate towards bicycles in France than they are in England, and there is only a charge of one penny to book a machine from one end of the country to the other, provided that your luggage does not exceed the weight allowed by the Company. In the event of your luggage being over-weight, as it most likely will be, you will find it will cost you about 45 francs to take a 'bike' out to Monte Carlo and back.

Fairly good machines can be hired on the spot, but most people prefer to ride their own, and if you intend spending a fortnight abroad, and riding most days, you will not save any money by hiring. Be careful to see that your brake is in good condition before starting; it will be fairly tested by some of the gradients you will encounter there, and an unreliable brake would mean positive danger in certain places.

If you have any regard for your health, you must take plenty of exercise at Monte Carlo. Most people take none; they order the richest dishes on the *menu*, over-eat themselves twice a day, remain in the poisonous atmosphere of the gambling-rooms for hours and hours at a stretch, and then wonder why they get out of sorts!

Frank's system was just the contrary. Weather permitting, he always had a good ride or walk during the day, ate a light lunch, and remained in 'the Rooms' as short a time as possible, and then always at the least crowded time, viz. from 5.30 to 8 p.m., when all the French and Germans are having their dinner. We found that by following this *régime*, we were ready to sample the best dinner that Monte Carlo could provide at eight o'clock, and were generally able to do full justice to it.

We never sat up very late at night, as we generally had to be up pretty early in the morning; the result was that ten days of this delightfully healthy existence made different beings of us both.

"We will settle to leave on December 21," said Frank; "by this means we shall escape the

Christmas holidays in London, and shall be able to stop in Monte Carlo over New Year's Day."

"All right," I said, "I'll leave all the travelling arrangements to you, and am ready to start any day that you care to fix."

"Then you had better get your bankers to pay in £300 to the London agents of Smith's bank, Monte Carlo, for your credit there, so that when we arrive, we shall find our capital all ready at hand, and shall not have the bother or risk of taking it out with us.

"Smith's bank is an English establishment," continued Frank, "where you will be treated with the greatest courtesy, and many a poor unfortunate punter can testify to their kindly assistance in the hour of need."

There is a popular belief that if a player loses all his money at the tables, the Administration of the Casino will always provide him with funds to leave the place. This used to be done freely until about five years ago, when a new Board of Directors took office. These gentlemen at once proceeded to adopt a policy of rigid economy, little in keeping with the old traditions of the place.

Time was, when you could go to Monte Carlo, live like a fighting-cock at the Hôtel de Paris for far less than it must have cost them

Ten Days at Monte Carlo

to keep you; you could hear some of the finest music in Europe, absolutely gratis, and if you lost all your money, you were promptly handed a ten-pound note, and bowed politely out of the place without any fuss.

Now, if you drink champagne for dinner, you can't live in the Principality under about £4 a day: for four months in the height of the season the free concerts are almost suspended, and the orchestra utilized for Operas, for which they charge you twenty francs for a seat: if you win at the tables the croupiers are bothering you all day long for gratuities, and if you lose all your money, well, you've got yourself into a mess, and you may get yourself out of it, for all *they* care. If you apply to the Administration, you have first got to swear that you have lost over £300; they will then take you round the Rooms like a criminal, in order that the croupiers at the tables where you have played may identify you and confirm your statement.

If the result of this investigation is satisfactory, the signatures of two directors must be obtained before anything further can be done. After this you are photographed, and once more taken round to be shown to all the doorkeepers, who are then given orders not to admit you any more. Next, you have to sign a promissory note for the amount of your travelling expenses,

Press Subventions

and instead of giving you the money, you are told that an employé of the establishment will meet you at the station at such and such an hour, and hand you a second-class ticket to your destination.

The consequence is, that rather than submit to all these indignities, most people prefer to visit Messrs. Smith and Co., who can get you out funds from any part of the United Kingdom in a few hours' time, provided you can prove your identity, and have credit at home.

After the music-loving public and the cleaned-out punters, the next people to suffer from the economies of the new Board were the representatives of the Press.

It was always a recognized thing that the Press had to be squared, and as much as £30,000 a year used to be given away in subventions.

There was a regular list kept of the different amounts to be paid at the beginning of each winter season, to the various local and Paris papers, and it was an understood thing that every paper on the list undertook to suppress all accounts of scandals and suicides in Monte Carlo.

I believe it was a fact that one of the most prominent of the Paris 'dailies' drew a big sum annually on these conditions, and also undertook to insert a paragraph on the front page, whenever the weather was particularly disagreeable in Paris, to the effect that the sunshine on the Riviera was 'merveilleux,' and the temperature at Monte Carlo 65° in the shade!

The proprietor of the same paper is reported to have sent his card up to the Director-General of the Casino one evening, informing him that he was in Monte Carlo for a few hours, and would like to amuse himself: would they kindly send him down 10,000 francs to play with? Having been duly handed the money he went into the Rooms, lost about 500 francs, and departed by the next train, leaving a polite message of thanks for the so-called loan, which of course they did not dare to reclaim from him.

Eventually this species of blackmail by the Press grew to such dimensions, that the Administration, like the proverbial worm, was forced to turn.

Fresh newspapers used to spring up at Nice every winter, and armies of newspaper proprietors, editors, and reporters called upon the Casino authorities annually, asking for various sums as hush-money.

But the climax was reached when a Company was formed at Nice, with the sole object of

Blackmailing the Casino

blackmailing the Gambling Establishment. They rented a plot of ground in one of the most frequented thoroughfares of the town, close to the Railway-station, on which they erected an enormous hoarding, about fifty feet high and fifty yards long. On this were depicted the scandals of Monte Carlo. You saw the gaily-dressed crowd thronging up the steps of the Casino, then the scene changed to night, and you saw the ruined gambler coming out with a look of desperation on his face and a revolver in his hand. He shoots himself, and the next picture depicts his widow and children discovering his body by moonlight on the terrace. The last picture, and the largest of the series, was the interior of the Palace of Monaco; the Prince was seated on his throne, with the Princess by his side, whilst the Casino employés were bringing in bags and bags of gold and laying them at his Highness's feet!

As soon as the show was ready, the Administration were duly invited to inspect the exhibition, and were told that it would be taken down on payment of 100,000 francs!

As they did not jump at this generous proposal, the Company had men stationed all down the street in which the pictures stood, distributing handbills drawing attention to them and recounting many harrowing occurrences which were supposed to have taken place in Monte Carlo within the last year or so.

Still the Casino did not 'rise,' and the end of it was, that the blackmailers went bankrupt, and their works of art were seized by the creditors and confiscated.

It was also the custom to give a banquet to the leading Press representatives on the night of the great Pigeon Shooting competition, and the story goes that every invited guest, on taking his place, found a thousand-franc note artfully concealed in his napkin!

It was doubtless easier for them to write of the admirable arrangements made for the comfort of visitors and the invariable courtesy shown by the management, etc., etc., after a dinner at which such liberality prevailed.

But now all this has been done away with, the Press subventions have been reduced to less than half the original figure, and the amount thus expended is looked upon purely as an advertisement, and not as hush-money.

The Casino has either become more independent, or has found that the Press has grown to such dimensions of late years that it is impossible to deal with it as formerly.

CHAPTER IV

Hints for the Journey—The Train de Luxe—The Yankee and his distinguished Card-sharper—Climate of Monte Carlo—Ciro and Ciro's Restaurant—Lunch at Ciro's—First Day's Play.

THE only way to travel to Monte Carlo expeditiously and with comfort is by the Train de Luxe. This is a vestibuled train composed entirely of sleeping cars, and a restaurant car, which runs right through from Calais to Vintimille—on the Italian frontier—about three times a week. The places are limited, and should be booked at the office of the International Sleeping Car Co., in Cockspur Street, at least ten days or a fortnight in advance. If your party consists of either two or four, you can secure an entire compartment, and can either take your own provisions with you, or take your meals in the restaurant car.

There is no trouble with the Custom-house if you travel by this service; the hand-luggage being examined on your arrival at Calais, and the heavy baggage in the luggage-van *en route*. You will not find them exacting at either place, and Frank and I easily smuggled through 400 cigarettes, and a couple of hundred cigars.

A little civility backed up by a five-franc piece here and there, goes a long way in France. Tip every one, and tip liberally, was our motto, and we met with politeness and courtesy everywhere.

We left Victoria at 9 a.m., had a very good crossing, considering the time of the year, and arrived at Monte Carlo punctually at 9.45 the next morning. This is not bad travelling, when you come to consider that the distance is close on 950 miles.

The supplementary fare for the Train de Luxe is £4 19s. 10d. over and above the first-class ticket; this is of course absurdly high, but all things considered it is well worth the extra money.

Our train was quite full, the passengers being almost entirely composed of M.P.s, City men, and barristers going out for the Christmas holidays. There were several card-parties going on, principally amongst the barristers, and Frank and I took a hand in a whist-party.

This reminds me of rather a good story of a very distinguished member of the legal pro-

Yankee and 'Card-sharper'

fession, who is as well known at Newmarket and other sporting resorts as he is in the Queen's Bench Division. He is likewise well known as a first-class card-player, and is never happier than when so engaged.

Last year an American friend of Frank's was travelling from Paris to Nice by the night Rapide, and found himself alone in a compartment with our legal friend.

They had not been *en route* more than two or three hours before X. (as we will call him) proposed a little game of cards, just to pass away the time. The American, having seen his name on his handbag, and thinking at the time that he looked all right, acquiesced, and they started at 8.30 p.m. to play *écarté*. When they arrived at Nice at nine the next morning, they were still playing, and when they came to settle up the Yankee found himself to be a loser of about £30. He then took it into his head that he had been swindled by a card-sharper, and immediately on reaching his hotel, wrote a letter to the Paris edition of the *New York Herald*, narrating his experiences, and warning people against playing cards with "a most respectable-looking old gentleman, masquerading under the name of X., as he was undoubtedly a professional, travelling card-sharper!"

Frank, who came to lunch with him—having

seen X. arriving at Monte Carlo an hour before —was only just in time to prevent the letter from being posted, and was easily able to convince his friend, by a minute description, that he had in reality been playing all night with a very eminent personage indeed!

On our arrival it was pouring with rain, and as we had discovered on the way out that most of our fellow-travellers were also going to our hotel, we at once made a rush for the Métropole 'bus. The hotel is quite close to the station, but when it does rain on the Riviera, there are no half-measures, and one would have been fairly drenched in three minutes.

It so happened that this rain was the luckiest thing that could possibly have occurred. We had not intended to take any exercise on the day of our arrival, and were consequently delighted to see the roads being well washed by a thorough good downpour.

"If it is fine to-morrow," said Frank, "the surface will be just perfect for 'biking' by ten o'clock," and so in fact it was.

It is rare to have rain at this time of the year at Monte Carlo, and for the remainder of our visit the weather was simply perfect.

Blundell, who met us at the station, told me that the most reliable months of the whole year are November and December. It is then bright and sunny, and the air is dry and bracing.

In January and February the weather is very uncertain and liable to 'Mistral'—a strong north-west wind which often continues for several days.

In March you get a hot sun but very cold east winds, which makes the climate most treacherous. April is nice but often cold, and in May you are liable to the 'Sirocco'—a hot enervating wind, which comes straight across the Mediterranean from the Great Sahara.

However, if you wish to see the country in all its beauty, you should certainly pay it a visit about May 10. Every house is then a blaze of colour, clothed with masses of pink and red ivy-geranium, varied occasionally by the orange of the nasturtium, and the purple of the lovely bougainvillea: every hedge is a bower of roses, the may and laburnum are in full bloom, and the whole air is laden with the perfume of the daphne. If you go out into the country, every field and every bank is a flower-garden, whilst at night the firelies flit around, and the nightingales sing you to sleep. May is beautiful enough in England, it's true, but on the Riviera it's like fairy-land, and must be seen to be fully realized.

Having arrived at the Hôtel Métropole, and

been duly introduced to Monsieur Varnier, the genial manager, we were escorted to our rooms, which had been reserved by Frank, about a fortnight in advance. They were on the third floor, facing full south, looking right on to the Casino Gardens, with the Mediterranean below.

The sun came streaming into our bedrooms at about seven o'clock every morning, and the view from our windows—which we were fortunate enough to see on two occasions—of the full moon rising out of the sea from behind Cap Martin, and throwing a great silvery path across the Bay of Roquebrune, was as fine as anything I have ever seen.

"We have just got a couple of hours," said Frank, "to make ourselves comfortable, and then we will go round and have lunch at Ciro's. We shall then soon see who is at Monte Carlo."

Ciro's restaurant, which is the most fashionable resort at luncheon-time, is most conveniently situated for visitors to the Métropole, as it is actually next door, and being on a covered terrace, one does not have to face the rain at all on a wet day.

Ciro himself is quite a character, and is certainly one of the most successful men that I know. Everything that he touches seems to turn to gold.

He is a Neapolitan by birth, and has been everything in his time, from bottle-washer to cook, and from bar-tender to restaurant proprietor. He served his apprenticeship in America, and was for some time at Delmonico's. He then came back to Europe, and it was a lucky day for him when he accepted the post of bar-tender at a little American bar on the Place du Casino at Monte Carlo.

From that day he began to go steadily ahead, and though it is not much more than ten years ago, he is now the sole proprietor of a good-sized bar—which is managed by his brother—and of one of the most fashionable restaurants in the world, to which he and Madame Ciro give their whole attention.

Ciro's motto is 'The very best,' and he certainly endeavours to live up to it. He says: "Some people say that my prices are too high, but if you want the best of everything, you've got to pay for it. I buy only the very best things in the market, and 'primeurs' at no matter what cost."

His charges certainly are rather heavy at times, but I personally have always found him very reasonable, and he contrives to keep his customers in a good humour by his witty replies and his funny English.

The following is an example of what he can

do. Frank and I went in to have an egg-nog at about ten o'clock one morning. The drinks were duly mixed, and disposed of. "How much?" we asked. "Five francs," said the bar-man. So we sent for Ciro, and Frank gently remonstrated with him. "We've had two egg-nogs, Ciro," he said. "I suppose they contain two eggs at about twenty centimes each; we will put the old brandy at one franc fifty, and the milk and the other etceteras will bring the cost up to just two francs; don't you think you are making rather an exorbitant profit on the transaction?"

"Yes, but you see," explained Ciro, "I know if you drink that *now*, you won't want so much lunch, so I'm bound to charge customers a lot for a drink like that!"

This ingenious explanation being greeted with roars of laughter from the bystanders, we had nothing left to do but to pay up and look pleasant.

But on one occasion Ciro himself came off second best. He had been interviewed by a correspondent of the *New York Herald*, on the subtle art of making cocktails, about which there had recently been some correspondence in the paper. Ciro was full of his subject—only metaphorically, of course—and showed proper scorn for the methods of some of the correspondents, who, he said, were evidently London and Paris bar-men, "most of whom know no more about mixing drinks than you do, and ought to be still washing glasses behind the bar; but I learnt my business with Jerry Thomas." He then proceeded to give *his own* recipe for the proper manufacture of a cocktail.

When the interview duly appeared in the *Herald*, one of his former employés, who had started a bar of his own in Paris, was very indignant at the aspersions cast on the Paris bar-men, and wrote to the Editor as follows:

" Dear Sir,

"Don't you believe what Ciro says; he never was with Jerry Thomas in his life, and as for 'his own' recipe, he copied it from a book which he keeps in a drawer behind the bar!

"Yours respectfully,

"George.

"*Rue etc., etc., Paris.*"

It will be a long time before Ciro hears the last of that book, 'in the drawer behind the bar.'

At luncheon-time at Ciro's, on a wet day, you can see all the notabilities in Monte Carlo compressed into a space of about twenty yards square. We had luckily sent Blundell down early to engage a table, for when we arrived the place was crammed full.

At a table in the window, the Grand Duke Michael and the Countess Torby were entertaining the Duke and Duchess of Connaught and the Crown Prince and Princess of Roumania. At the next table the Lord Chief Justice and Lady Russell were breakfasting with their son and daughter-in-law, and one or two members of the Junior Bar.

Next to them Mr. George Edwardes and Mr. Jewitt were lunching with Sam Loates and Sloan, the little American jockey, who was a most comical sight sitting next to the portly form of 'Gaiety George.' A well-known Lombard Street banker had a cheery party of ladies, whilst amongst his male guests we made out Mr. 'Charley' Bulpett and Mr. C. F. Gill.

The legal and political element was very strongly represented. Mr. Carson and his wife were in one corner of the room, whilst the Speaker of the House of Commons and Mrs. Gully had a small party in another. Sir William Walrond, the popular Conservative Whip, was talking to Lord Onslow.

Art was represented by Mr. Charles Wertheimer and Mr. Morland Agnew; the Stage by Miss Miriam Clements, 'La Belle Juniori,' and

Fanny Ward; Music by Tosti and Sir Arthur Sullivan; and Sport by Messrs. Douglas Baird and Harry McCalmont.

London Society was also well to the fore, and amongst the best-known we made out Mr. and Mrs. Wm. McEwan, Captain and Mrs. 'Ronny' Greville, Lord and Lady Wolverton, Lord and Lady 'Algy' Lennox, the Duke and Duchess of Leeds, Sir John Willoughby and Mr. 'Monty' Guest. If you add to all these, a sprinkling of superbly dressed *demi-mondaines*, some foreign notabilities, a few barristers, City men, and stockbrokers, you will have a very fair idea of Ciro's restaurant during the Monte Carlo season.

We found Blundell a most useful guide, he knew everything and everybody. We left the ordering of the lunch to him, and right well he did us. We were four altogether, as I had invited a City friend. The *menu* was as follows:

Hors d'Œuvres variés.
Œufs pochés Grand Duc.
Mostèle à l'Anglaise.
Volaille en Casserole à la Fermière.
Pâtisserie.
Fromage.
Café.
Vins et Liqueurs.
Château Carbonnieux, 1891.
Fine Champagne, 1846.

Ten Days at Monte Carlo

The Mostèle is a speciality of this part of the world, and is the most prized of the Mediterranean fish. It is very like a whiting, only much more delicate. Split open, filled with butter and bread-crumbs, and fried, they are delicious. I also recommend to your notice the Château Carbonnieux; it is a very superior Graves, and should be slightly iced. It mixes well with any mineral water, and is the nicest breakfast wine that I know.

To give you an idea of Ciro's prices, I append the bill:

CIRO'S RESTAURANT, MONTE CARLO.

	fcs.	c.
4 Couverts	2	
Beurre Isigny	1	
Hors d'Œuvres variés	2	50
6 Œufs pochés Grand Duc	4	50
Mostèle Anglaise	8	
Volaille Casserole	12	
Pâtisserie, Gateaux	2	
Fromage Brie	2	
4 Café filtre	4	
4 Fine Champagne, 1846	8	
1 Magnum Carbonnieux, 1891	15	
Total	61	00

Seeing that we were four persons, and that the coffee, wines, and liqueurs alone come to 27 francs, I think you will agree with me that the eatables are not overcharged, considering that this is one of the best restaurants in Europe. We found that when we were alone, if we avoided

General Rules for the System

expensive wines and liqueurs, we could lunch for 7 francs 50 cents., and dine for 10 francs a head.

After a cigar, we paid a visit to Smith's Bank next door, drew out our capital of £600, and then strolled across to the concert at the Casino. This lasted till 4.15, and at 5 p.m. we made our first onslaught on the Bank.

It may here be as well to remind the reader of the General Rules for playing the System.

1. Always back the colour that came up *last but one*. 'Zero,' representing neither colour, is treated as no 'coup.'
2. When 'Zero' appears, exercise the right of taking half your stake off the table, and place it to a separate account. The total amount to the credit of 'Zero Fund' is added to your profits at the end of the day. The 'coup' is scored as a loss.
3. When the score reaches—
    - − 10 increase your unit to 2
    - − 30 ,, ,, ,, 3
    - − 60 ,, ,, ,, 4
    - − 100 ,, ,, ,, 5

    and continue playing with the increased stakes until all losses are retrieved. Then re-commence staking one unit.
4. Continue playing until you can show a net profit of Fcs. 400 or over.

Ten Days at Monte Carlo

We determined to play every day at the same table, and after looking round carefully, came to the conclusion that the table in the third room, on the right-hand side, appeared to be the least frequented. After looking on for about a quarter of an hour, we secured two seats, and the table ran as follows:[1]

FIRST DAY'S PLAY.

Contractions in Tables: St.= Stake, L= Lose, W= Win.

Black.	Red.	Score.	Black.	Red.	Score.
	14	No Stake	4		−6
	9	No Stake			1 W
33		St. 1 L		12	−5
26		1 L			1 W
	9	−2 1 L		3	−4 1 L
	21	−3 1 L	17		−5 1 L
	36	−4 1 W		32	−6 1 W
11		−3 1 L	Z.		−5 1 L
15		−4 1 L		14	−6 1 L
	9	−5 1 L		19	−7 1 W
		−6			−6

[1] N.B.—We commence staking on the third spin.

First Day's Play

Black.	Red.	Score.	Black.	Red.	Score.
4		−6 1 L	22		−8 2 W
17		−7 1 L	4		−6 2 W
	3	−8 1 L	6		−4 2 W
26		−9 1 W	24		−2 2 W
	Z.	−8 1 L	10		0 1 W
33		−9 1 L			+1
35		−10 St. 2 W	11		1 W
		−8	10		1 W

ZERO FUND.   SUMMARY.
Fcs. 50 on 14th coup   Coups played . 30
    50 ,, 21st   ,,   Won . . . 14
   ───   Lost . . . 16
   100   Units won . . 3
   ═══

3 units @ fcs. 100 = fcs. 300
Add Zero Fund . . .   100
            Total won .   ───
                          400
                          ═══

It will be seen, that on the 23rd 'coup' the score being − 10, we increase our unit to 2, and on the 28th spin, having retrieved all our losses, we reduce it again to 1. Zero having turned up twice, we take off fifty francs each

51

time, and place it to a separate account, reckoning the 'coup' as lost.

We now come in for a nice run on the Black, and after three more spins, we are able to retire, having won three units, there being now 100 francs to the credit of 'Zero Fund.' The *séance* lasted just three-quarters of an hour.

After this, we dressed and dined quietly at the Métropole, and after one more stroll across to 'the Rooms' to inspect the evening toilettes, we retired early to bed, to sleep off the effects of the journey down.

CHAPTER V

First Bicycle Ride—La Crémaillère—La Turbie—Corniche Road—Valley of the Paillon—Èze—Cap Martin—Lunch at Cap Martin Hôtel—Second Day's Play.

WE both agreed not to make our rides too long at the commencement of our visit, as neither of us had been doing any 'biking' for the last two months, and we wished to get gradually accustomed to the hills.

"We will go up to La Turbie by the train," said Frank, "take a ride of about four miles in the direction of Nice, then turn back and run down to Cap Martin for lunch. After lunch we will ride quietly home."

The ancient village of La Turbie stands just behind Monte Carlo, at an altitude of about 1700 feet, but it is made charmingly accessible by means of the little mountain railway, known as 'La Crémaillère,' which takes you up in exactly twenty minutes; fare, second-class, 2.30 francs, and no charge for bicycles. Take my advice and

Ten Days at Monte Carlo

go second, as the first-class compartments are stuffy.

The gradient at the start is most alarming, and one cannot help wondering what would happen should the engine break down, but after the first half-mile it becomes all plain sailing.

We stop once on the way up, at the pretty little station of Bordina, and have two minutes to admire the fine view below us, and the station-master's charming flower-garden.

It is just below this that the International Sleeping Car Company are building another of their large hotels; they have chosen a beautiful site, well sheltered from the wind, and doubtless the establishment, when finished, will be as popular as their Riviera Palace at Nice. The inauguration takes place, I believe, on January 1st, 1899.

On arriving at the top, about fifty yards from the station, is a semi-circular sort of balcony, built right on the edge of the precipice, and from here the finest view is obtained.

Monaco and Monte Carlo lie right at our feet, and it looks as if one could easily throw a stone either on to the Casino or into the pretty little harbour, which can now boast of three or four steam-yachts. To the north-east is the picturesque village of Roquebrune, nestling against the side of the mountain, while to the east are Cap

Martin and Mentone, with Bordighera in the distance.

It was from this spot, about two years ago, that Frank saw a great race between the *Britannia*, *Ailsa*, and *Satanita*, and from his description it must have been a truly wonderful sight. The Bay of Roquebrune filled with thirty or forty small raters—looking in the distance like toy ships on the Serpentine—the three big yachts tearing through their midst with a fine breeze behind them, and the sun shining on the harbour, now full of steam-yachts of every nationality, all dressed with bunting in honour of the occasion. From this commanding spot, with the aid of a good glass, one could follow every detail of a yacht race.

We reluctantly tear ourselves away, and entering the village of La Turbie, turn to the left, and ride right through the village. The road descends as far as a bridge over a small gorge, and then steadily rises for about three kilomètres. I may here mention, that to bring kilomètres to miles (roughly), you multiply by 6 and divide by 10; in other words, ten kilomètres equal approximately six English miles.

We now get a fine view of the ancient and interesting old village of Eze, which stands right on the top of a cone-shaped mountain, below us on our left. We are here at the very highest point of the Corniche Road, roughly speaking about 2000 feet above the sea.

Should you wish to explore the village of Eze, I advise you to leave your 'bikes' out of the question, train from Monte Carlo to Eze-sur-Mer, and walk up from there by the steep footpath to the village. This takes about an hour and a quarter. You can afterwards walk from there to La Turbie, and descend by the railway to Monte Carlo. This makes a very nice little excursion on a fine cool day.

The day being clear, we now get a fine panorama to the west, which we were unable to see from La Turbie, owing to the mountain, known as the Tête de Chien, intercepting the view. Beaulieu and Cap St. Jean lie at our feet, Villefranche and Nice beyond, with the beautiful Esterel range away in the far distance.

From this point the road descends the whole way to Nice, and the first mile and a half is as pretty a bit of 'coasting' as I know of anywhere, except perhaps from the top of Hinde Head, on the Portsmouth Road, down into Godalming. The descent is gradual, the road wide, and the surface absolutely perfect. After a run of about six minutes, with our feet up all the way, we arrive at our destination.

We pass two auberges, one on the right-hand side of the road, and the other on the left, and

View from the Corniche Road

it is here that the carriage-road branches off to Eze. We continue for a hundred yards or so until we come to another road leaving the Corniche, on the right-hand side; this is only a short cut to Nice and joins the main road again, about two miles below. It is too steep and too rough to be rideable with comfort.

But here was the view that Frank had brought me to see, and it certainly repaid us for climbing the ascent from La Turbie. The obstruction to our right being now removed, the whole of the country to the north and north-west comes suddenly into view, and is spread out like a map at our feet. The beautiful valley of the Paillon, with the little village of Trinité Victor, is immediately below us, with the mountains behind, rising gradually higher and higher and culminating in a magnificent range of snow-clad peaks. On a bright clear day this is worth going miles to see.

From here to the Cap Martin Hotel is just about twenty kilomètres, but about sixteen of it being downhill, one can ride it very easily in an hour and ten minutes. There is some safe 'coasting' as far as La Turbie, but after that, I strongly advise you to keep your feet on the pedals. A girl on her honeymoon was nearly killed through reckless riding on this road only last year.

About nine kilomètres after leaving La Turbie, the Corniche passes close under the village of Roquebrune, and joins the lower road from Monte Carlo to Mentone. About fifty yards from this junction, on the Mentone side, there is another very fine view.

If you stand against the wall, facing the sea, you have got the whole of Cap Martin spread out at your feet, and can easily make out the Empress Eugénie's fine Villa Cyrnos, which is the fourth visible on the right-hand side, the first, belonging to Captain Wentworth, being almost hidden amongst the trees. On our right is a magnificent view of Monte Carlo, Monaco, and the Tête de Chien, and on our left the whole of Mentone is now visible.

We continue down the hill towards Mentone, until we come to the Barracks, and then take the first turning to the right. This brings us on to the sea front, and turning again to the right, we enter the Cap Martin Estate, and in five minutes time arrive at the hotel.

This establishment, started about six years ago by Mr. Colvin White—the owner of Cap Martin —and a few friends, including Mr. Edward Smith, the Monte Carlo banker, has had a most phenomenal success. The Prince and Princess of Wales stopped there for some weeks the first year it was opened, and since that time it has been honoured by Royalty of some sort every year.

Mr. Ulrich, the popular manager, has been twice decorated by the Emperor of Austria, and it is reported that the chef knows more different ways of serving up eggs than any man in Europe. They give you a most excellent *table d'hôte* lunch, at separate tables, at a reasonable price.

After lunch, and a stroll round the gardens, we started for home, and turning sharp to the left, on leaving the hotel, kept along the west side of the Cap, and passed the gates of the Empress's villa. The ride back to Monte Carlo takes about thirty-five to forty minutes; the hills, with the exception of one very steep little bit, being mostly in the right direction. One has to ride carefully on entering the town, as the electric tramway has made the road rather dangerous for cyclists.

On arriving at the Métropole, we changed our clothes, had some tea, and then prepared for the business of the day. As it turned out, we were in for a considerably longer *séance* than on the previous day, but by means of the system and plenty of patience, we were returned victorious, after a struggle of rather more than two hours.

The table ran as follows :

Ten Days at Monte Carlo

SECOND DAY'S PLAY.

Black.	Red.	Score.	Black.	Red.	Score.
26	Z.	No Stake		23	−4 1 L
		No Stake			
17		No Stake			
22		+1 W	33		−5 1 W
31		+1 W		18	−4 1 W
	3	St. 1 L			
	7	1 L		21	−3 1 L
4		−2 1 L			
8		−3 1 L		36	−4 1 W
	25	−4 1 L		34	−3 1 W
24		−5 1 W	28		−2 1 L
	32	−4 1 W	8		−3 1 L
	27	−3 1 L	10		−4 1 W
11		−4 1 L		21	−3 1 L
	9	−5 1 W		1	−4 1 L
		−4 1 W	33		−5 1 L
6		−3 1 L	17		−6 1 L
10		−4			−7

Second Day's Play

Black.	Red.	Score.	Black.	Red.	Score.
	34	−7 1 L	6		−20 2 L
	9	−8 1 L	8	18	−22 2 W
20		−9 1 L			−20 2 L
15		−10 St. 2 L	17		−22 2 W
	27	−12 2 L	31		−20 2 L
	16	−14 2 L	13		−22 2 W
28		−16 2 L	22		−20 2 W
	18	−18 2 W	Z.		−18 2 L
11		−16 2 W		34	−20 2 L
4		−14 2 L		23	−22 2 L
15		−16 2 W	17		−24 2 L
	12	−14 2 L		5	−26 2 W
	14	−16 2 L		19	−24 2 L
10		−18 2 L		32	−26 2 W
		−20			−24

[61]

Ten Days at Monte Carlo

Black.	Red	Score.	Black.	Red.	Score.
	34	−24 2 W		30	−33 3 L
	9	−22 2 W	29		−36 3 L
20		−20 2 L		27	−39 3 W
	16	−22 2 W	11		−36 3 W
	19	−20 2 L		25	−33 3 W
10		−22 2 L	8		−30 3 W
	23	−24 2 W		32	−27 3 W
8		−22 2 W	4		−24 3 W
20		−20 2 L	24		−21 3 L
	7	−22 2 L	29		−24 3 W
	14	−24 2 L	22		−21 3 W
15		−26 2 L	13		−18 3 W
17		−28 2 L	24		−15 3 W
	19	−30 St. 3 L	6		−12 3 W
		−33			−9

Second Day's Play

Black.	Red.	Score.	Black.	Red.	Score.
2		− 9 / 3 W		3	− 9 / 3 W
	18	− 6 / 3 L	28		− 6 / 3 W
	Z.	− 9 / 3 L		36	− 3 / 3 W
31		− 12 / 3 W			0
		− 9			

ZERO FUND.

Fcs. 100 on 49th coup
150 ,, 86th ,,
250

SUMMARY.

Coups played   90
Won   . . 41
Lost   . . 49
Units won . 2

2 units @ fcs. 100 = fcs. 200
Add Zero Fund . . 250
Total won . 450

It will be seen that we win two units, the first two spins played, but after that we play 88 'coups' without winning another. On the 31st 'coup' we increase our unit to 2, and on the 69th—the score being − 30—we increase to 3, and are at one time as much as 39 units to the bad. After this, a run of intermittence and a sequence of eight Blacks, followed by another intermittence, enables us to win back all our losses, and as there is a sum of 250 francs to the credit of 'Zero account,' we are able to retire with a win of 450 francs.

CHAPTER VI

Second Bicycle Ride—Monte Carlo to Nice—The Legend of Sainte Dévote — Beaulieu — Villefranche — The 'London House'—Third Day's Play—Concert at the Casino—The Monte Carlo Orchestra.

THE ride from Monte Carlo to Nice, by the lower road, is rather hilly, but the gradients are so good that a strong rider need not dismount at all. A rider of this calibre would take about an hour and a quarter from the Hôtel Métropole to the Place Masséna, a distance of exactly thirteen miles.

We, however, intend not only to walk up the steep places, but to stop occasionally to admire the series of beautiful views which the road continually presents; we shall consequently allow ourselves rather more than two hours.

The Condamine Hill being now dangerous on account of the Electric Tramway, we leave Monte Carlo by the upper road, across the Bridge of Sainte Dévote. Below us, on the left, is the curiously situated little Chapel, which owes its existence to the following romantic legend.

Dévote, a Christian by birth, lived in Corsica at the time of the persecution of the Christians, under the Emperors Diocletian and Maximilian. She was seized by the Roman Governor and called upon to offer sacrifices to the pagan gods, but as she stoutly refused, they put her to every conceivable torture, thinking to make her obey. All these she cheerfully endured, continuing to pray fervently, and to offer up thanks to God that the honour of martyrdom had been conferred upon her.

At last, a voice from the clouds proclaimed that her prayers were heard, and a dove flew out of her mouth and soared heavenwards. Her body, which had been ordered by the Governor to be burnt, was rescued by two Christian priests during the night, who, with the assistance of a sailor named Gratian, embalmed it, placed it in a boat, and set sail for the coast of Africa. But a strong south wind sprung up, and drove them northwards. All night long they toiled and struggled against the elements, but it was useless, and with the utmost difficulty they kept themselves afloat.

At last Gratian, utterly exhausted, fell asleep, and during his slumber the spirit of the martyr

Legend of Sainte Dévote

appeared to him: "Cease battling against the wind," she said, "the gale will soon abate. In the morning you will see a dove come out of my mouth, follow it to land, and wherever it alights, there bury my body." In the morning the dove duly made its appearance, and leading them into what is now the little harbour of Monaco, alighted on the spot where the Shrine stands.

This being supposed to have occurred on January 27, that day is still kept as a religious festival in the Principality; and a very pretty and interesting sight it is, to see the long solemn procession wending its way from the Cathedral at Monaco to the little Chapel under the railway bridge to do homage to the memory of the martyred saint.

After leaving the bridge, the road continues to descend for about one kilomètre, until we come to the Cemetery, on our right, which stands at the extreme limit of the Principality. We now come to the frontier, and have a long ascent of about two kilomètres to negotiate. The gradient, however, is not very severe, and it is quite rideable all the way.

About half-a-mile from the Cemetery, we arrive outside Sir Edward Malet's new Château, with its two imposing-looking Lodges, on the right-hand side of the road. We will here stop for a moment to admire the lovely view behind us. This is one of the most picturesque views of the little Principality.

The 'singular sea-girt rock' of Monaco, with its old-world Palace and modern Cathedral, stands boldly out in the foreground, with part of Monte Carlo visible to the left, and the rugged mountains beyond; the whole making up a most charming picture.

We are now at the village of Cap d'Ail; the Pigeon Shooting Ground is on our left, down by the sea. On our right we soon come to the enormous Villa Sanitas, formerly an hotel, but now used as a villa by the Countess van der Osten; in April and May the walls are almost entirely hidden by masses of ivy-geranium, and the garden is a beautiful sight.

Below us, on our left, a little further on, is the Eden Hotel, which has just been re-opened, after remaining closed for a great many years. It is under new management, and bids fair to become popular. About half-a-mile further up the hill on our right, is the charming Villa des Terrasses, which was occupied last year by the Dowager Empress of Russia and the young Cesarewitch. The latter, whose lungs were supposed to be in a very dangerous condition, used to sleep out on the verandah, covered in by an awning, all through the month of March.

Beaulieu

His sojourn of three months in this Villa proved very beneficial to his health.

A short distance further on we ride through two tunnels, and have now reached the top of the hill. From this point to the station of Eze is all on a descent. About a mile below the tunnels we cross a bridge, and just above it is the old Monastery of St. Laurent d'Eze, at present uninhabited—having been recently purchased, together with a large area of land behind, by Sir Edward Malet.

From the station of Eze to the commencement of Beaulieu is almost on the flat, and then the road once more begins to rise.

The first striking object that we meet with in Beaulieu is the imposing-looking Hôtel Bristol, at present in the course of construction, under the auspices of Sir John Blundell Maple. Leaving this on our left, we ascend the road leading to Beaulieu station, and now have a fine view of Lord Salisbury's Villa 'La Bastide,' perched on the hill, just above the village, and looking like a large Swiss châlet.

At Beaulieu station we turn to the left, and the road continues to rise gradually, until Villefranche Harbour comes into view, when the gradient becomes rather tiring, and the latter part of this hill had better be taken on foot. Below us, on the left, at the corner of the bay, is Mr. Harry McCalmont's new villa, with an

unpronounceable name, but easily recognized by
the white ensign floating on the turret.

We mount our machines at the top of the
hill, and can now ride straight on to Nice without
again dismounting. The road descends
sharply on to the Place d'Armes—where the
crews of the men-of-war in the harbour may
often be seen at drill—and then rises again, but
with a very easy gradient. Two miles further
on we reach the top of the Mont Boron Hill,
and from here there is a truly magnificent view
of the entire town and environs of Nice. The
old fashioned 'Port' and the Quai Lunel are
just below us, backed by the Castle Hill; to the
south-west is the entire length of the Promenade
des Anglais, with the Esterel Range in the far
distance, while to the west and north-west is
the town of Nice, with Cimiez rising in the background.
The huge Regina Palace, where the
Queen has spent the last two winters, is unmistakably
visible on the hill, and although about
four miles distant, gives one a fair idea of its
immense size.

The descent into the town is quite two kilomètres
long, and is a fine bit of riding, when the
roads are in good condition. On arriving at the
Port we turn sharp to the left, which takes us
on to the sea-front, and another five minutes
brings us to the Place Masséna.

There are four first-class restaurants in Nice,

Lunch at the London House

the London House and the Français being very good and decidedly expensive, whilst the Helder and the Regence are good and more reasonable in price.

Having still the greatest confidence in our system, we decide to try the London House, and a very excellent lunch they gave us. This establishment is quite on a par with Ciro's at Monte Carlo, and the charges are relatively about the same.

There is a very good bicycle shop almost opposite the Restaurant, where they are only too pleased to take charge of your machines, and give them a dusting over during lunch.

The London House is always filled with the *monde chic* at luncheon time, but the *clientèle* is decidedly more cosmopolitan than at Ciro's, where about seventy-five per cent. of the people are usually English. Here, we have a strong Parisian element, mixed with Italians, Austrians, Russians, and a fair number of Americans. After coffee and cigars, we take a short stroll on the Promenade des Anglais, and then make a start for home.

Passing the 'Port,' we notice a goodly array of steam-yachts moored alongside the quai, the most noticeable being Mr. Vanderbilt's *Valiant* —probably the largest private yacht in the world—and Mr. Higgins's beautiful *Varuna*, both of course flying the Stars and Stripes. The Mont Boron Hill is quite rideable, but is tiring, owing to its great length, and we recommend most riders to walk a portion of it.

On reaching the summit, after about two kilomètres on the flat, the road bends round to the left, and we get a very fine view of Villefranche harbour, picturesquely situated as it is in a sort of natural amphitheatre. Should you have the good luck to see it when the Queen is at Cimiez, and there are two or three English men-of-war lying at anchor, alongside the French Mediterranean Squadron of about fifteen enormous vessels, with perhaps two or three large private steam-yachts besides, you will probably agree with me, that it is a magnificent spectacle.

After passing the Place d'Armes, there is rather a stiff hill, which had better be walked, and then we have a clear run to the station of Eze. Between Beaulieu and Eze, on emerging from a tunnel, where the road curves round to the left, there is a splendid view of the village of Eze, but the outer walls of it are built so much in configuration with the mountains around, that if you did not know where to look for the village, you would hardly notice its existence.

After passing the station at Eze we have another longish hill to be surmounted before we reach the tunnels at La Turbie, and then it is

Third Day's Play

all plain sailing into Monaco. The view, half way down the hill, which we admired so much in the morning, is now even more beautiful in the rays of the setting sun. The ride back from Nice to Monte Carlo takes rather longer than it does to go, as the steep hills are against one most of the way. If the rider should be tired, he can always take the train at Beaulieu, and thereby avoid two of the stiffest ascents.

Having shaken off the dust of the road, and changed our clothes, we sallied forth to the Casino, and took our seats at the usual table about half-past five. The numbers came out as follows:

THIRD DAY'S PLAY.

Black	Red	Score
8		No stake.
4		No stake.
	16	Stake 1 Lose
33		1 Win
		0
	3	1 W
		+ 1
20		1 W
8		1 L
31		1 W
		0
13		1 W
		+ 1
29		1 W

ZERO FUND.
Nil.

SUMMARY.

Coups played . . . 8
Won 6
Lost 2
Units won 4

4 units @ fcs. 100 = fcs. 400
Add Zero Fund ,, 0
Total won 400

Ten Days at Monte Carlo

It will be seen that we are in great luck to-night, and just happening to come in for an intermittence of four, followed by an unfinished sequence of five Blacks, we are able to retire with 400 francs, after a *séance* of exactly twelve minutes. We consequently decided to dine early, at the *table d'hôte* at the Metropole, and go to the concert, as the programme for that evening seemed to be particularly attractive. There are free concerts at the Casino twice a-day, except when the Operas are being performed, viz. from about January 1 till the end of March, when there are only about five free concerts per week. Besides these there is a very fine classical concert every Thursday afternoon, when they make a small charge for seats.

The Monte Carlo Orchestra is one of the most famous in the world. From November to May it consists of eighty permanent musicians, of whom about thirty-five are competent soloists. In the summer months the strength is reduced to about fifty, but the men who leave in May all return in November, after doing a short season with another orchestra, either at Aix-les-Bains or Biarritz. The result is, that this large body of picked musicians, having played together for years under the same leadership, have attained a very high standard of perfection.

In Monsieur Léon Jehin, they have got a very

The Monte Carlo Orchestra

able conductor, who has done much to raise the level of the concerts during the last few years. It is quite a treat to see him conduct; he seems to know every note of the music, without referring to the score, and to throw his whole soul into the execution of it. Even if one were deaf it would be a pleasure to see him conducting a piece like the overture to '*Tannhäuser*.' The following was the programme for the evening:

CERCLE DES ÉTRANGERS DE MONACO

CONCERT

Sous la direction de M. Léon JEHIN

MM. Gaétan BORGHINI et Louis VIALET Sous-Chefs

SOLOISTES DE L'ORCHESTRE

Mlle THÉVENET et M. ROOS, harpistes—MM. CORSANEGO, COMTE et BOURDAROT, violons—NACHTERGAELE et ZAVATTARO, altos—Carlo SANSONI et TERZOLO, violoncelles—FRANCHI, contrebasse—GABUS, CHAVANIS et BERGIN, flûtes—DOREL, LAVAGNE et SIANESI, hautbois—PROUVEN, CAUBÉRE et SAINTE-MARIE, clarinettes—SEIGLE et ESPAIGNET, bassons—BRICOUX, LHOEST et BONTOUX, cors—CHAVANNE, DELSA et DUCLAUD pistons—VAN EESSEN, RIKIR et DE CAMILLIS, trombones—ASE, bombardino.

À 8 heures et demie du Soir

Zampa, ouverture	*Hérold*
Pizzicati	*Gillet*
Fantasie sur La Favorita	*Donizetti*
Valse de Concert	*Godard*
Overture de Tannhäuser	*Wagner*
Berceuse de Jocelyn	*Godard*
(Solo de Violon par M. Corsanego)	
Dernier sommeil de la Vierge	*Massenet*
Amoretten-Tanze, valse	*Gung'l*

The Monte Carlo Orchestra

The accuracy and precision of the strings in the 'Pizzicati' was something marvellous. In 'La Favorita' the brass was heard to great advantage, while the execution of the lovely overture to '*Tannhäuser*' was simply perfect.

Monsieur Corsanego, the first violin, is a great acquisition to the band; he is a very effective soloist, with perfect tone and fine execution. He is, moreover, the fortunate possessor of a valuable Straduarius, reported to be the gift of a rich lady admirer. In the lovely 'Berceuse de Jocelyn' he was quite at his best, and of course scored a rapturous encore.

After the concert, we took a turn round the Rooms, to inspect the new arrivals, and wound up the evening with a whisky-and-soda at the American Bar of the Café de Paris.

CHAPTER VII

Third Ride—La Turbie—The Monastery of Laghet—'Ex Votos'—The Gold-embroidered Slippers of the Comtesse de B——.—Laghet to Nice—St. Jean—Cap St. Hospice—Fourth Day's Play—A Triumph for the System.

THE rides and drives starting from Monte Carlo are naturally very limited in number, as the place itself is situated, as it were, on a shelf, and there is only the road into Italy to the east and the road to Nice on the west. It is not advisable for the cyclist to go into Italy, for two reasons: in the first place, even though you may be a member of the Touring Club de France, they give you no end of trouble at the Custom-house on the frontier; and in the second place the roads are very inferior.

We decided, therefore, to confine ourselves to French territory, and by making constant use of the little railway to La Turbie, and occasionally using the P. L. M., we found that we could

The Augustan Trophy

'explore a new bit of country every day, and could doubtless have continued to do so for nearly a month.

To-day, we again have recourse to the little 'Crémaillère,' and going up by the 9.30 a.m. train, reach La Turbie before ten.

This time, we take a stroll through the old part of the village, and inspect the remains of the Roman Monument. If history is to be believed, this tower must originally have been something gigantic. It was built by Augustus Cæsar in the year A.D. 8, to commemorate a crushing defeat he had just inflicted on the surrounding tribes. A portion of it was destroyed by the Moors in the sixth century, and finally the Duke of Berwick caused the monument to be undermined, and blown up, in the year 1705. Why he should have committed this act of Vandalism I have been unable to ascertain. It is said, that from the ruins of the Augustan Trophy, not only the church and almost the entire village of La Turbie have been constructed, but a considerable quantity of the stone has also been taken down and used for building purposes in Monaco itself; and yet there is still enough of it left standing to make a very imposing ruin! At any rate, Tennyson seems to have been sufficiently impressed by it, to write the lines—

> "What Roman strength Turbia showed
> In ruin, by the mountain road."

The church, and the old portion of Turbia, are doubtless worth exploring from an antiquarian and artistic point of view, and it is certainly cleaner than most places of its kind.

We leave La Turbie by the same road as that described on page 55, but near the bottom of the hill, about a quarter of a mile outside the village, we find a road branching off to the right, marked:

"Sanctuaire de Laghet, 2 kil."

Taking this road, which should be carefully ridden, as the gradient is steep, and the turns very sharp in places, we soon arrive at the Monastery.

Most picturesquely situated at the head of a pretty little valley running due west to the Paillon, and entirely sheltered by mountains to the north and east, this fine building looks more like an old château than a monastery. Its history is as follows: the votary chapel and convent were built by the Carmelites in the seventeenth century. In 1704 it was deprived of its wealth—accumulated during sixty years—by the Princes of Savoy, who, being in financial straits, owing to war, were compelled to raise funds from the offerings brought by the faithful. In

1792, the French converted the convent into a hospital; but in 1815, when Piédmont resumed possession of its ancient territory, the Carmelites were re-installed at Laghet. Finally, in 1864, they bought the freehold from the French Government, as it had then become part of the new French Department of the Alpes-Maritimes.

On Palm Sunday, Trinity Sunday, or Whit Sunday, crowds of devotees, and pilgrims from all parts of the country, flock to the place, and the little courtyard of the monastery presents a most animated scene. Booths and stalls are erected for the sale of sweets, toys, relics, etc., and a lively trade is carried on.

In the interior of the building they have a most remarkable collection of votive offerings, or *ex votos* as they are called, principally consisting of pictures. These depict the most miraculous escapes from accidents, disasters, and afflictions of every kind. We see men falling off scaffoldings, children being run over, shipwrecks, surgical operations, and such like, all the victims being presumably either saved, or relieved, by the miraculous intervention of the patron saint. As the people in these illustrations, and more especially the animals, all bear a strong family likeness to one another, I presume they keep an artist on the premises who will turn you out an *ex voto* at so much a square foot. If this be so, he assuredly belongs to the ultra-realistic school!

But what attracted my attention more than all these works of art, was a dainty little pair of gold-embroidered slippers. They looked so strangely out of place, hanging over one of the doors close to the chapel, amongst an extraordinary collection of discarded crutches, surgical bandages, etc., etc. My curiosity was so aroused, that having approached one of the monks, I bought some relics from him, and over a glass of the rather nasty liqueur that is brewed on the premises, lured him on to tell me the history of the slippers. He proved equal to the occasion, and diving through one of the doors, he shortly re-appeared with a copy of the *Figaro* about four months old. In it was a story about three columns long, written in beautiful French, all about my little slippers. As I have never met any one yet who knew the story, I venture to reproduce it here.

About thirty years ago Comte de B——, a young man of good family, but impoverished through extravagance, was fortunate enough to win the affections of Mademoiselle P——, a beautiful Mentonese orphan, who, on coming of age, was entitled to a large fortune. They were duly married, but unfortunately it did not take the young girl very long to discover

A Romantic 'ex voto'

that the Count was not really in love with her, and had only married her for her money. He was a confirmed gambler, and used to spend all his time at the Monte Carlo tables, leaving her alone all day at Mentone. When he did return, late at night, he was generally in the worst of tempers, and the result was, that for four months they led a most miserable existence.

Being utterly wretched, the young Countess resolved to run away one day, whilst her husband was at Monte Carlo, to try if religion would bring any consolation. She accordingly disappeared one morning, and no one knew what had become of her. She had in reality gone to Laghet, and taken rooms at the inn there under an assumed name, and there she remained hidden for over three months, spending most of her time in prayers and devotions.

One day, the Count, having had terribly bad luck at the tables before lunch, resolved to go for a walk in the afternoon to cool his heated brain. He was now quite at the end of his resources, and was wondering what on earth he should do if he could not find his wife and win her over again.

He climbed the hill to La Turbie, and wandered aimlessly on to Laghet, and was sitting at a table outside the little inn drinking an absinthe, when all of a sudden a terrific storm commenced. It thundered and lightened and poured in torrents. After it had continued for over two hours without showing any signs of abating, the Count began to wonder what he should do. It was beginning to get dark, and here he was without a coat or even an umbrella, and there was not a carriage to be had within twelve miles.

There was no help for it, he would have to pass the night there. So he sent for the good woman who kept the inn and asked if they could put him up for the night. "Certainly, they had a bedroom which was at his disposal, but they were sorry there was no place where he could dine in comfort, as the only sitting-room in the house had been occupied by a lady for the last three months, and he would therefore have to dine in the kitchen or in his bedroom; unless, that is to say, Madame would permit him to dine with her in the parlour. If Monsieur would be so good as to give them his card, they would explain the situation to Madame, and see what could be done."

So his card was duly taken to the Countess, and the circumstances explained, and although the situation was decidedly embarrassing, there was no way out of it: she was occupying the room which was in reality the public dining-

A Romantic 'ex voto'

room, so she could not well refuse, especially as the Monsieur was described as being very nice-looking, 'avec un air très distingué!'

When the Count entered the room, and found that the lady who so kindly allowed him to dine in her sitting-room was in reality his own wife, his astonishment can be better imagined than described! She received him very coldly, and kept him quite at a distance during the whole of dinner, but as the night was intensely cold, and there was no other fire in the house, she could not well refuse to allow him to remain in the room until it was time to retire to bed. The Countess drew up her arm-chair to the fire, and the Count thought he had never seen his wife look so perfectly charming as she did that night, dressed in a most becoming peignoir, with the tiny gold-embroidered slippers on her dainty little feet.

For the first time in his life he fell genuinely in love with her, and throwing himself on his knees at her feet he implored her forgiveness. "If she would only come back to him, he would promise to give up gambling for ever. They would sell the house at Mentone and go to Paris, where he would find some occupation, and be out of the way of temptation."

Seeing that he was really in earnest, she of course forgave him, and they became reconciled on the spot. Two years afterwards, having lived happily ever since, and being now the mother of a little boy, born on the anniversary of their reconciliation, the Countess again visited Laghet, and in addition to a handsome donation to the funds of the Monastery, she left the gold-embroidered slippers as an *ex voto*. Such was the story as it appeared in the *Figaro*, and uncommonly well it was written.

But to get to Nice in time for lunch we must be going on, so we leave the courtyard of the Monastery, and, instead of crossing the bridge, turn down sharp to the left and double back under it. This is a rough and stony path for about a quarter of a mile, but if you do not care to wheel the machines yourself, you will find plenty of boys waiting on the bridge, who for ten sous will gladly undertake the job. After crossing a small stream, we find ourselves once more on a very good road, which descends with a gentle gradient all the way to the village of Trinité Victor. This is situated on the bank of the Paillon about seven kilomètres from Laghet, and on turning to the left, about another eight kilomètres will bring us into Nice. The principal objects to be noticed on the way down are the Observatory perched high up on the hill to our left, above the Corniche Road, whilst on our right we pass a large lunatic asylum, and

Cap St. Hospice

lower down the Monastery of St. Pons. The Monastery of Cimiez is also visible on the high ground to our right.

We ride straight on into the town of Nice, and crossing the river make for the Café de la Regence, which is situated at the corner of the Avenue de la Gare, and the Rue Hôtel de la Poste.

Here they provide you with a very good lunch, and the prices show a great reduction on those of the London House, but you will not find the company nearly so entertaining as at the latter restaurant.

After lunch, instead of riding straight back to Monte Carlo, as described in the preceding chapter, we take the road as far as Villefranche, and at the bottom of the hill after leaving the town, about two kilomètres from Villefranche and eight and a half from Nice, we turn off to the right across a bridge over the railway. This brings us right in front of Mr. McCalmont's villa, where we turn to the left, and continuing to bear away to the left, eventually arrive at the charmingly situated little fishing village of St. Jean.

Riding through the village, we continue on to a little promontory that runs right out to sea, commonly known as Cap St. Hospice. At the extreme point is a pretty little church and a

Ten Days at Monte Carlo

Martello Tower. It was in this little churchyard that the body of Paganini, the famous violinist, was first interred, but it was subsequently stolen from here by the Italians during the night.

From the Martello Tower there is a wonderful view of the coast-line to the east. From here to the point of Monaco is a magnificent semi-circular bay, surrounded by rugged mountains. The little village of Eze is in the centre perched up on high, whilst away to the east are Cap Martin, Vintimille, and Bordighera, in the far distance.

Retracing our steps we ride back to the village of St. Jean, where there are two restaurants, the Hôtel Namouna and the Restaurant de la Bouillabaisse, kept by one Marc Antoine. Both these hostelries are famous for 'Bouillabaisse,' the well-known Provençale delicacy, made of rock-fish and small langoustes, and flavoured with garlic. It is a most excellent dish for lunch.

From here to the Hôtel Bristol at Beaulieu, there is only a narrow path running along the sea-shore; this is quite rideable, with care, but should hardly be undertaken by a beginner. At Beaulieu we take the train for Monte Carlo, having ridden altogether about 35 kilomètres.

At six o'clock we took our seats at the Casino at the usual table, and on this occasion we had

Fourth Day's Play

an experience that fully demonstrated the strength of our system. Details of the play are appended:

FOURTH DAY'S PLAY.

Black.	Red.	Score.	Black.	Red.	Score.
	36	No Stake			− 7
	12	No Stake	33		1 W
29		St. 1 L			
6		1 L			− 6
				32	1 L
		− 2			
31		1 W			− 7
				12	1 L
		− 1			
	14	1 L			−8
			15		1 L
		− 2			
24		1 W			− 9
			8		1 L
		− 1			
10		1 L			− 10
					St. 2 W
		− 2	6		
	25	1 L			− 8
				14	2 L
		− 3			
	19	1 L			− 10
					2 W
		− 4	17		
13		1 L			− 8
					2 L
		− 5	29		
28		1 L			− 10
				5	2 L
		− 6			
	30	1 L			− 12
				3	2 L
		− 7			
6		1 W			− 14
				1	2 W
		− 6			
15		1 L			− 12
		− 7			

Ten Days at Monte Carlo

Black.	Red.	Score.	Black.	Red.	Score.
	21	−12 2 W		19	−12 2 L
6		−10 2 L		18	−14 2 L
2		−12 2 L	Z.		−16 2 L
13		−14 2 W	28		−18 2 L
29		−12 2 W	Z.		−20 2 L
	1	−10 2 L	17		−22 2 L
	16	−12 2 L	33		−24 2 W
	27	−14 2 W		18	−22 2 L
6		−12 2 L		30	−24 2 L
Z.		−14 2 L	4		−26 2 L
	25	−16 2 W	24		−28 2 L
4		−14 2 W	29		−30 St. 3 W
11		−12 2 L	22		−27 3 W
10		−14 2 W	13		−24 3 W
		−12			−21

Fourth Day's Play

Black.	Red.	Score.	Black.	Red.	Score.
24		−21 3 W	11		−18 3 W
6		−18 3 W		14	−15 3 L
	16	−15 3 L		30	−18 3 L
2		−18 3 W		14	−21 3 W
13		−15 3 L	8		−18 3 L
	12	−18 3 L		5	−21 3 W
	36	−21 3 L		3	−18 3 L
	16	−24 3 W		9	−21 3 W
11		−21 3 L		3	−18 3 W
	27	−24 3 W		36	−15 3 W
24		−21 3 W		25	−12 3 W
	18	−18 3 W		34	−9 3 W
28		−15 3 W		14	−6 3 W
2		−12 3 L		21	−3 3 W
	Z.	−15 3 L			0
		−18			

[91]

Ten Days at Monte Carlo

ZERO FUND.	SUMMARY.
Fcs. 100 on 35th coup	Coups played . . 82
,, 100 ,, 42nd ,,	Won 36
,, 100 ,, 44th ,,	Lost 46
,, 150 ,, 68th ,,	Units won . . . 0
Fcs. 450	Add Zero Fund, fcs. 450

The table runs very badly for us at the commencement, and it will be seen that at the 19th 'coup' we have to increase our unit to 2.

Our bad luck still continues, and at the 51st 'coup' being — 30, we increase the unit to 3. Meanwhile 'zero' has come up three times, and as we were playing stakes of 200 francs at the time, we have been able to take off 300 francs, and place them to 'Zero Fund.'

Our luck then commences to improve, till eventually, with a run of 9 reds, we are able to bring the score to O. Having by this time 450 francs to the credit of 'Zero Fund,' we can now retire with that amount in hand.

It will be seen, that although we have won more than our prescribed amount, the Bank has won 25 per cent. more bets than ourselves on that day's play.

Once more our system had triumphed !

CHAPTER VIII

Fourth Ride—Railway of the Sud de la France—Nice—Colomars—Tourettes—Vence—Cagnes—Fifth Day's Play—French 'as she is spoke' at the Tables—Restaurant of the Hôtel de Paris—Monsieur Fleury.

TO-DAY, we explore an entirely new country to the north-west of Nice. In addition to the river Paillon, which comes down from the mountains, and runs right through the centre of the town, there is another and still larger river, Le Var, which flows into the sea, about four miles to the west of Nice. There is an excellent road alongside the river, with hardly a hill worth mentioning, for at least forty miles, and as there is a most convenient little railway, which also follows the river as far as Puget-Théniers, 65 kilométres from Nice, the cyclist will be hard to please if he cannot arrange a ride to suit his taste.

This wonderful little railway, called the Sud de la France, starts from Nice to the north of the P. L. M., and runs right up into the heart of the mountains, and by its aid one is enabled to enjoy magnificent scenery, and arrive at the most interesting little villages, which would otherwise be inaccessible to the majority of cyclists. At a place called Colomars, about 17 kilomètres by road from Nice, this railway divides; one line continuing up the valley of the Var to Puget-Théniers, and the other crossing the river and going to Grasse and Draguignan. We intend to ride from Nice to Colomars, which is on the flat, and then take the latter line, after lunch, to a station called Tourettes, from whence we have a splendid run back into Nice.

We left Monte Carlo by the 9.40 a.m. train, and arrived at Nice soon after ten. On leaving the station you turn to the right, and then take the first to the left, viz. the Boulevard Gambetta, which brings you down on to the Promenade des Anglais. Here of course you turn to the right, and continue straight ahead, till you come to a railway-bridge close to the station of Le Var. Here the road divides, but *we* have to continue straight on under the bridge, and along the left bank of the river, till we come to the Colomars station, about 17 kilomètres from Nice.

Just outside Colomars station there is a very

good little *café* restaurant, kept by the representative of the Touring Club de France, and here they give you as good a lunch as any one requires, with wine *ad lib.* and coffee and liqueurs, for about 3.50 francs a head. From the road at Colomars there is a really magnificent view. The swiftly-running river is at our feet, the mountains surrounding it are studded with the most picturesque little villages, and far away to the north is a range of snow peaks. Just across the river to the west is the majestic Crag of St. Jeannet, with the quaint little village of that name nestling beneath it. This curiously-shaped mass of rock forms a well-known landmark, which can be seen for many miles in either direction. Looking up the valley, the little village of Gattières is perched up high on our left, Carros is in front, with Castagniers and Asprémont on the right.

Our train, which leaves at 12.35 p.m., crosses the river, and immediately makes a very stiff ascent to Gattières; we then pass close under St. Jeannet, run through Vence, and arrive at Tourettes at 1.42 p.m. This is a most curious old place, about 1100 feet above the sea, and although it has a railway-station, and is within sixteen miles of Nice, it looks as if it had remained in much the same condition for the last thousand years or so. We take a stroll through the village, and then mount our machines and ride to Vence, about five kilomètres distant, on the road to Nice.

Vence is a place of some importance, having considerably over 3000 inhabitants. It is the seat of a Bishop, and can therefore boast of a cathedral, which dates back to the fifteenth century. From an architectural and antiquarian point of view, I should think there are few more interesting places than this in the whole neighbourhood.

From Vence, down on to the high road running from Cannes to Nice, is a splendid run of about nine kilomètres, with a descent of nearly 1000 feet; the road is wide, with a fine surface, and is nowhere sufficiently steep to be dangerous. After descending for about four and a half kilomètres, we pass the ancient town of Saint Paul, which stands on a hill away to our right. The road now descends through pine woods, until about three kilomètres further on we have a fine view of the old town of Cagnes, situated on an eminence to our left, with its grand old Grimaldi Castle in the centre. We enter the modern part of the town, and turn to the left, where we find ourselves on the Route Nationale, which brings us to Nice after another twelve kilomètres on the flat. There is nothing of much interest to be noticed on the way from

Fifth Day's Play

Cagnes to Nice with the exception of the view from the bridge crossing the Var. Shortly after passing the bridge the race-course may be seen on the right-hand side of the road. On arriving at Nice we have some tea, and then take the train to Monte Carlo. We have ridden to-day about 43 kilomètres.

We went over to the Casino at about six o'clock, and found that we had a very easy day's work before us. The table ran as appears on page 98.

Zero comes up the very first spin, and is followed by two more losses. We then find that we are on a run of six Blacks, and are therefore enabled to win our first unit. The table then gives us five Reds, which enables us to win another unit, and as we now come in for an unfinished run of four intermittences, we are able to retire on the 16th 'coup' with 450 francs. The *séance* only lasted twenty-five minutes.

We were very much amused at the behaviour of a most excitable Englishwoman, who was playing at our table. She knew about as much French as the ordinary school-boy of ten, and her pronunciation of what little she did know was so extraordinary that she would probably have been better understood had she stuck to her native tongue. It is usual when one wishes to change gold into five-franc pieces to pass the

FIFTH DAY'S PLAY.

Black.	Red.	Score.	Black.	Red.	Score.
	3	No Stake		32	1 L
	23	No Stake		18	1 L
29	Z.	St. 1 L 1 L		3	−2 1 W
31		−2 1 L		14	−1 1 W
10		−3 1 W		36	0 1 W
17		−2 1 W	29		+1
26		−1 1 W		34	1 L 1 W
10		0 1 W	4		0 1 W
		+1		12	+1 +1 W

ZERO FUND.

Fcs. 50 on 1st coup.

SUMMARY.

Coups played 16
Won 10
Lost 6
Units won 4

4 units @ fcs. 100 = fcs. 400
Add Zero Fund . . . 50
Total won . . 450

croupier a louis, and ask for 'quatre pièces.' Instead of this she kept passing up louis from the end of the table, and asking in a loud voice for 'quatre morceaux, s'il vous plaît.' She appeared quite unconscious that every one at the table was laughing at her; and, on one occasion, having given the croupier a piece to put on 8, which she thought he had wrongly placed, she shrieked out, as the ball was spinning, "Croupier! croupier! je vous avvay dee de mettay le morceau sur le 'wheat,' mais vous l'avvay mettay sur le 'ongs'!" Unfortunately for her the 'wheat' did not come up.

Curious mistakes often occur through the extraordinary pronunciation of French by the English people in 'the Rooms.' On one occasion a friend of Frank's who wished to change a thousand-franc note into hundred-franc pieces, had been told to ask for 'plaques.' He accordingly went up to one of the croupiers, handed him the note, and said, "Plaques, s'il vous plaît." There was rather a crowd at the tables, so he did not notice what the man was doing, and was very much astonished when, after some delay, he was handed back two thousand francs! The croupier, thinking our friend was talking English, had put the note on to *Black*, which, fortunately for him, turned up, otherwise there would have been no end of a fuss.

This reminds me of another amusing incident that occurred last year at Monte Carlo.

Lord Salisbury was ill with influenza, and a most alarming telegram had been posted up in the Hall of the Casino in the morning, to the effect that his lordship was very much worse, and would probably have to resign office. About five o'clock in the evening B——, one of the biggest gossips and busybodies in the place, rushed into the hall of the Métropole, where about fifty people were having tea, and shouted out, "Have you heard the news? Lord Salisbury has gone mad!"

Of course there was tremendous excitement; people rushed up-stairs to tell their friends and relations, and the news spread like wildfire.

"How did you hear it?" I inquired rather sceptically. "Oh, there can be no doubt about it," he said; "I saw the telegram myself at the Rooms. It has just been posted up." Rather doubting B——'s ability to translate a French telegram correctly, I thought I would stroll across and see what it said. The message was: "La dernière nouvelle de Lord Salisbury est démentie." This he had construed into "the latest news *is* that Lord Salisbury is demented!"

As the system was going so successfully, and we were living well within our means, we decided to indulge to-night in an expensive dinner at the restaurant of the Hôtel de Paris, which every one informed us was 'one of the sights of the place.'

Although Ciro's is 'the very best' place for

Dinner at 'The Paris'.

lunch in Monte Carlo, it is by no means the most amusing restaurant for dinner. It is perhaps the most *comfortable* place to dine at, as the service is always good, and there is no crowd, but many people would consider it too quiet. Undoubtedly the finest, largest, and most amusing place for dinner is the restaurant of the Hôtel de Paris. It is the most beautiful room in Monte Carlo, and every night, probably from February 1 till April 15, they serve at least seven or eight hundred dinners. The cellar is certainly the best in the place, and would probably compare favourably with any establishment of its size in the world.

The general excellence of the restaurant is undoubtedly entirely due to the energy and great ability of Monsieur Fleury, the manager. If Ciro can be compared to a brigadier, Fleury should take rank as general of a division, for he has at least four times the staff to control, and four times the number of clients to serve, and yet he contrives to please them all. He has the best of good manners, a most amiable disposition, and plenty of tact. They say he draws the largest salary of any hotel manager in the world, and as he has probably more than doubled the receipts of the Paris during the last three years, he no doubt deserves it.

What an extraordinary collection of human

beings you find assembled here at about half-past eight o'clock! Princes, Grand-Dukes, aristocrats of every nationality, diplomates, financiers, politicians, actors, and even jockeys, are all busily engaged in discussing the good things which 'le Bon Dieu,' through the medium of Mons. Fleury, has been pleased to provide. And the ladies; well, this is the place to see *them* in all their glory! Some, no doubt, take an interest in the good things also, but what the majority are chiefly engaged upon, is in displaying the smartest frocks and the latest hats, provided by their long-suffering husbands—or somebody else's husbands—through the obliging medium of Messrs. Doucet and Worth; and likewise in criticizing those of their neighbours!

The actresses and *demi-monde* here reign supreme, and are arrayed in all their war-paint. You will see Liane de Pougy, La Belle Otero, and the beautiful Madame Martial, covered with jewels: Fanny Ward, Mathilde Damuseau, and the charming Madame 'Lula' always dressed to perfection; and if you are lucky, you may perhaps catch a glimpse of the famous Princesse de Chimay.

We gave Mons. Fleury *carte blanche* to order us a nice little dinner, only stipulating that it should not be too long. The following is what he gave us:

Monsieur Fleury

Hors d'Œuvres.
Consommé à la Reine.
Filets de Merlan Bercy.
Selle d'Agneau Renaissance.
Bécasse Rôti.
Salade.
Soufflé Surprise.
Vins.

Moet and Chandon, Dry Imperial, 1889.
Cuvée, 36.
Fine Champagne, 1809.
Grande Réserve.

The fish *à la Bercy* is one of the specialities of this restaurant, and is equally good with sole, merlan, or *mostèle*. It is a most delicious sauce, flavoured with the little native onions, called *échalotes*. The *soufflé surprise* is also a speciality of the Paris. The *soufflé* comes up steaming hot, and with all the appearance of an ordinary *soufflé*, but when you come to help yourself, you find that the centre consists of delicious strawberry or raspberry ice! How on earth they manage to serve it without the ice melting, is a culinary mystery that I am unable to solve.

Fleury is a great connoisseur of wine, and prides himself very much on the old brandy at the Paris. We asked for a couple of glasses of the very best in the house, and found it very much to be recommended. It is four francs a glass, ninety francs a bottle, or £30 a dozen!

Ten Days at Monte Carlo

If you go over the cellars, they will show you one huge cask of old brandy, which is said to be worth nearly 100,000 francs!

To give you an idea of the charges at the Paris, a copy of our bill is appended.

Hôtel de Paris, Monte Carlo.

	fcs.	c.
2 Couverts	1	
Hors d'Œuvres	1	50
Consommé	2	50
Merlan	5	
Selle d'Agneau	5	
Bécasse, Salade	10	
Soufflé	4	
Café	2	
1 Moet and Chandon, 1889, frappée	19	
2 Fine Champagne, 1809	8	
Total	58	00

CHAPTER IX

Fifth Ride—Grasse—Fragonard and his famous Panels—Magagnosc—Villeneuve-Loubet—Sixth Day's Play.

THE two finest rides within easy reach of Monte Carlo are undoubtedly from Grasse to Nice, and from Entrevaux to Colomars. In both cases you take the train up into the mountains, and return on your 'bikes,' through a beautiful country, along a road with a perfect surface, and a slight gradient in the right direction, almost the entire distance.

The most picturesque line to Grasse is of course the Sud de la France, *viâ* Colomars, Tourettes, and the Gorges du Loup, but as the first train started from Nice too early for us, and as the second one gets to Grasse too late in the day, we decided to go by the P. L. M. line *viâ* Cannes.

We particularly wished to get to Grasse in good time, as we had, through the courtesy of

Messrs. Smith and Co., the Bankers, obtained permission to view the famous pictures of Fragonard, in the old house of M. Malvilan. This, as it turned out, was a great piece of good luck, for the pictures, after having remained exactly as we saw them for just upon a hundred years, were sold three weeks after our visit, and we were consequently almost the last foreign visitors to view them.

Most useful and ever-obliging people are Smith and Co. They will provide you with funds 'to break the Bank,' and remit your winnings home to England; they will book you places in the train, and give you a ticket for almost any destination on the face of the globe; they are House Agents, Estate Agents, Insurance Agents, and Wine Merchants; and in this particular instance they seem to have acted most successfully as Agents for a dealer in works of Art.

For the last twenty-five years the Art Dealers of the whole world have been trying to buy those famous pictures at Grasse without success; and when, a few years ago, the somewhat eccentric owner showed the door to an amateur, who brought 800,000 francs with him and placed the notes on the table of his *salon*, it was generally supposed that money would not buy the Fragonards, at any rate during the lifetime of M. Malvilan.

Fragonard's Pictures

Messrs. Smith and Co., however, appear to have succeeded where so many had failed, and thanks to their intervention, the pictures are, at the time I write, safely removed and duly installed in London.

Leaving Monte Carlo at 9.40 a.m., and changing the train at Cannes, you arrive at Grasse in time for lunch. The best thing to do on arrival, is to put your 'bikes' on to the Grand Hotel 'bus, and go up in it yourselves to the hotel. It is nearly two miles from the station to the Grand, with a very stiff ascent for most of the way, so it is certainly not advisable to attempt to ride it.

Having lunched extremely well at this excellent hotel, from the terrace of which there is a truly delightful view, we proceeded on our machines to the house of M. Malvilan. The old gentleman himself was, I regret to say, indisposed, and unable to receive us, but being accompanied by Messrs. Smith and Co.'s representative at Grasse, who had very kindly met us at the Grand Hotel, we were at once admitted and shown the pictures.

It may here interest the reader to learn something of Fragonard, and these five most famous paintings.

Jean Honoré Fragonard was born at Grasse in 1732, and began life seriously, at the age of fifteen, as a notary's clerk. As, however, he soon found himself quite unfitted for the legal profession, and had always shown much artistic talent, he was sent up to Paris with an introduction to Boucher.

The latter appears to have taken a great fancy at first sight to the fresh young Provençal boy, and a genuine and lasting affection sprung up between them. 'Frago' (as Boucher used to call him) proved himself such an apt pupil, that at the age of twenty he carried off 'the grand prix de Rome' with his 'Jeroboam sacrificing to Idols.' Inspired by his success, he determined to visit Italy, and study in the Italian Schools. Before leaving, Boucher warned him not to take the great Italian Masters too seriously, as he was convinced, at the time, that it was in the lighter style of painting that his pupil would excel. 'Frago' was absent from Paris for about five years, and when he returned he attempted the treatment of more serious and ambitious subjects. As, however, he could find no sale for such works, he finally adopted his master's style, which was exactly suited to the taste of the period.

On Boucher's death, in 1770, Fragonard became the most popular painter of the day, and being possessed of charming manners, and plenty of wit, he readily obtained the *entrée* to the society of the Court. For some years previous to the Revolution he was making as much as sixty thousand francs a year by his brush. A great French critic has said : " Si Boucher était le peintre des nymphes, Fragonard aura été celui de l'Amour et du Baiser."

Shortly before her death Madame du Barry commissioned Fragonard to paint her four large panels for the decoration of the *salon* of her Château de Louveciennes. The paintings were duly executed, and represented a love story : they were entitled, 'La Rencontre,' 'La Déclaration,' 'La Sérénade,' and 'L'Escalade.' Then the King died, and Madame du Barry being unable to take delivery of the panels, they were consequently thrown upon the artist's hands. Fragonard made many attempts to sell them without success, and still possessed them when the Revolution broke out.

He then went down to Grasse on a visit to his old-friend the Marquis de Blys. He told his friend about the panels, and the latter, in spite of the hardness of the times, was tempted to take them off the artist's hands at a nominal figure. Fragonard consequently went back to Paris and brought down the panels to Grasse, and they were duly installed in the *salon*, where we had the good fortune to see them.

As soon as they were set up, Fragonard noticed that a fifth panel was necessary to complete the decoration of the room, and he accordingly set to work to paint another, which is called 'L'Abandon.' This, unfortunately, was still unfinished at the time of his death, or it would certainly have been the most beautiful of the series.

It is reported that the price paid by the Marquis for the five great pictures was only fifteen hundred francs, but as both he himself and the artist were in great poverty at the time, owing to the Revolution, this was a matter of arrangement between them.

With the commencement of the nineteenth century, pictures of the Boucher and Fragonard School went quite out of fashion, and there being no further demand for his works, poor 'Frago' died in the year 1806 in abject poverty. Such is the irony of Fate!

The Marquis de Blys lived for a great many years after Fragonard's death, and though almost penniless, turned a deaf ear to all would-be purchasers of his magnificent *chef d'œuvres*. He took a great pride in showing them to visitors, and it must have been a touching sight to see the broken-down old nobleman in this poor little house, ill clad, with a hat full of holes, living like a pauper rather than give up the paintings, which he considered as part of the family. He died, not so very long ago, at a

The Fragonard Paintings

great age, urging his daughter, who had married M. Malvilan, to have "neither his pride nor his madness." But times improved, and the Malvilans, though never rich, became comfortably off. Madame Malvilan died leaving a daughter, who also died young, leaving two little girls; and if M. Malvilan had not been advised that it would be in his grandchildren's interests to sell, he also would probably have died in possession of the pictures. As it is, he reluctantly consented to sell them to Mr. Charles Wertheimer, of Norfolk Street, London, for the sum of fifty thousand pounds, on condition that the purchaser allowed him eight months in which to have the panels copied.

This has now been done, and the copies, which are a great success, may be seen in the *salon* which contained the originals.

Of course the moment the sale became known, there was a great outcry in the French papers against 'Perfide Albion,' who was said to be robbing France of her choicest works of art. The *Figaro* alone took a broad view of the transaction. In a leading article it said that the sale was a subject for great congratulation for France, for it would undoubtedly enhance the value of French pictures in the markets of the world. Mr. Wertheimer, with his accustomed generosity, would be sure to lend his new treasures to one of those marvellous exhibitions that take place annually in London. Thousands of people would flock to see pictures which had such an interesting history, and for which such a fabulous price had been paid, and the public would thus have the opportunity of comparing the works of a French artist, comparatively unknown in England, with the Dutch, Italian, and English Schools of the same period. Such a comparison could not fail to be favourable to France.

It is not difficult to discover that the principal industry of Grasse is the manufacture of perfumery and scented soap. The whole town smells like the Strand outside Rimmel's shop, and if one had the time to spare, a visit to one of the factories would doubtless be very interesting. I believe that about one-fifth of the scent used in the entire world now comes from the little town of Grasse; in addition to which they export annually large quantities of preserved fruits and prussic acid, made from the kernels of the bitter almonds. A great number of the roses used for the manufacture of the famous Otto of Roses are cultivated on the slopes between Grasse and Cannes. From the middle of April till May 15, this whole tract of country, of several square miles, resembles one enormous rose-bed.

On leaving M. Malvilan's house, we again ride up past the Grand Hotel, and continue to ascend for about 4½ kilomètres to a village called Magagnosc. On our right about a mile from the Grand Hotel is a lovely Château with large private grounds, belonging to Baroness de Rothschild, who has lived at Grasse for a great number of years. Beyond it there is a fine view down the valley to the sea, with the Esterels closing in the view to the west.

The ascent to Magagnosc is very gradual and easily ridden, as the surface of the road is perfect. After passing through the village there are several cross-roads, and we must be careful to take the right one: fortunately there can be no mistake, as there is a sign-post with 'Route Nationale, No. 85' plainly marked on it. This is our best way to Nice, as we wish to get back to Monte Carlo in time for the business of the day. If one had another hour or so to spare, the most picturesque road is the one branching off to the left, just outside Magagnosc, leading down through the 'Gorges du Loup' to Le Bar, and then ascending to the village of Tourettes, from whence the ride would be the same as described in the preceding chapter. The scenery the whole way is very fine, but there is a long hill of over five kilomètres to be surmounted between Le Loup and Tourettes, and it will take an ordinary rider about an hour longer to reach Cagnes by this route.

From Magagnosc to Villeneuve-Loubet is a gentle descent the whole way for about $17\frac{1}{2}$ kilomètres. There is safe 'coasting' for most of the distance, if your machine is provided with a good reliable brake. The views are somewhat restricted as the valley is a narrow one, and the road runs for part of the way through pine-woods. On arriving at Villeneuve-Loubet, we stop for a moment on the bridge to admire the fine modern Château, standing on a hill in the centre of the village. A short way below the bridge on the right bank of the river is an excellent country inn, where they will provide you with lunch or tea at very moderate rates. They are famous for their trout, caught in the Loup. This is a charming place for a picnic dinner from Nice in the month of May, as the woods all round the inn are full of nightingales. From Villeneuve to Cagnes is only about three kilomètres, but there is one stiff hill to ascend, part of which had better be walked. From Cagnes to Nice is all plain sailing on the flat. The whole distance from Grasse to Nice is about 36 kilomètres, and will take an ordinary rider about two hours. As it was, we just caught the 5.25 p.m. train from Nice, which brought us to Monte Carlo

Sixth Day's Play

before six. We were in our seats at the table by 6.40, which is perhaps the very best time of the whole day for playing a system. There are so few people gambling then, that you will often see over fifty spins in the hour as compared with about thirty at half-past four in the afternoon or ten o'clock at night. The numbers came out as follows:

SIXTH DAY'S PLAY.

Black.	Red.	Score.	Black.	Red.	Score.
35	5	No Stake		19	−3 1 W
	16	No Stake St. 1 W		25	−2 1 W
28		St. 1 W		19	−1 1 W
26		St. 1 L		1	0 1 W
15		1 W			+1
	5	0 1 L	10		St. 1 L
29		−1 1 W	20		1 L
8		0 1 L	6		−2 1 W
	32	−1 1 L		27	−1 1 L
	30	−2 1 L		14	−2 1 L
		−3			−3

Ten Days at Monte Carlo

Black.	Red.	Score.	Black.	Red.	Score.
	19	$-3 \atop 1$ W		30	$-9 \atop 1$ W
4		$-2 \atop 1$ L		7	$-8 \atop 1$ W
26		$-3 \atop 1$ L		27	$-7 \atop 1$ W
	16	$-4 \atop 1$ L		23	$-6 \atop 1$ W
	9	$-5 \atop 1$ L		34	$-5 \atop 1$ W
	12	$-6 \atop 1$ W		16	$-4 \atop 1$ W
10		$-5 \atop 1$ L		14	$-3 \atop 1$ W
26		$-6 \atop 1$ L	26		$-2 \atop 1$ L
	19	$-7 \atop 1$ L	24		$-3 \atop 1$ L
	34	$-8 \atop 1$ L	31		$-4 \atop 1$ W
	3	$-9 \atop 1$ W		34	$-3 \atop 1$ L
29		$-8 \atop 1$ L		32	$-4 \atop 1$ L
	30	$-9 \atop 1$ W		16	$-5 \atop 1$ W
	36	$-8 \atop 1$ L		32	$-4 \atop 1$ W
		-9			-3

Sixth Day's Play

Black.	Red.	Score.	Black.	Red.	Score.
	7	-3 1 W		9	-1 1 W
10		-2 1 L		25	0 1 L
28		-3 1 L	33		-1 1 L
2		-4 1 W	28		-2 1 L
	30	-3 1 L	24		-3 1 W
22		-4 1 W	20		-2 1 W
	1	-3 1 W	13		-1 1 W
4		-2 1 W	17		0 1 W
		-1			+1

Zero Fund.

Fcs. 0

Summary.

Coups played . . . 60
Won 32
Lost 28
Units won 4

4 units @ fcs. 100 = fcs. 400
Add Zero Fund .   0
Total won . 400

We win two units on the first two spins, and a third one on the 13th 'coup,' but the winning of the fourth one takes us just another hour's play. The reason of this is, that our luck is never sufficiently bad to allow us to double our unit. We get to −9 on the 28th 'coup' and again on the 30th, but from that moment we begin to make up our ground, still playing stakes of one unit. Zero does not help us at all to-day, as it never appears during the whole *séance*. On the 60th 'coup' we at last win the fourth unit, and find that we have been just an hour and twenty minutes at the table. Feeling rather tired, we had a quiet dinner at the Métropole and went to bed.

CHAPTER X

Sixth Ride—Peillon—Peille—Pic de Baudon—Seventh Day's Play—Restaurant of the Grand Hotel—François.

I WONDER how many, out of the hundreds of thousands of people who annually visit Monte Carlo, have ever seen the little village of Peillon. I don't suppose one in ten thousand have ever heard of it, and certainly not one in twenty thousand have ever arrived there. And yet for the picturesqueness of its situation, and for the general beauty of the scenery surrounding it, I know of no place of easy access in the neighbourhood that surpasses it.

As the crow flies, Peillon is not more than four miles due north of Monte Carlo, and the most direct way to arrive there is undoubtedly on foot from La Turbie: but with the aid of the 'Crémaillère,' and by making use of the footpath at Laghet, it also makes a very charming excursion for cyclists.

Ten Days at Monte Carlo

As we shall not be near any restaurant at lunch-time, it is best to strap a packet of sandwiches on to the handle of your bicycle before starting on this expedition; you can also slip a flask of whisky-and-water into your pocket, though this is not really necessary, as we shall pass several Buvettes on the way, where very drinkable native wine can be obtained.

The best way for pedestrians making an excursion of this kind, if their party consists of half-a-dozen people, including ladies, is to take up a luncheon-basket in the train to La Turbie, and have it strapped on to a donkey. There are two or three men with donkeys there, who are accustomed to carrying lunch and acting as guides at the same time. There are several splendid walks to be made, starting from La Turbie; the one to Peillon and Peille, and then down into Mentone *via* Gorbio, being an exceedingly beautiful expedition, though rather long; and there is another fine walk right round Mont Agel and down to Cabbé Roquebrune Station. The air on these mountains is most invigorating, and the scenery on a clear day superb.

We take the train to La Turbie and ride from there to Laghet, where we find a couple of boys to help to carry our machines down on to the road to Trinité Victor, exactly as described on

Peillon

page 86. I hear, by the way, that they contemplate making the quarter of a mile required to join these two roads at an early date, when the expedition here described will become possible for carriages.

On arriving at Trinité Victor, we turn to the right and continue up the left bank of the river Paillon, till we come to the village of Drap (pronounced Drappe), about one kilomètre from where we turned into the main road. We ride on through Drap, and continue for about another kilomètre and a half, till we come to a fine bridge crossing the Paillon, which flows down a valley on our right, and joins a large tributary here.

Immediately after crossing this bridge, we turn to the right and ride up this valley. The road is marked No. 21, so there can be no mistake about it. We are now in one of the most charming little valleys of the whole neighbourhood. It is rather narrow in places, but beautifully wooded : the road is also narrow but with a very fair surface, and a gradient against us, which is almost imperceptible. There is an air of restfulness and peace about this little valley which is irresistible, and one feels for a few miles at least that one has left the haunts of the 'scorcher' and the 'petroleum fiend' behind. Turning a corner about two miles and a half from the main road, the little village of Peillon suddenly comes into view. Perched on the crest of a mountain, which rises up from the centre of the valley, it seems to all appearances as inaccessible as an eagle's nest.

And by this time the traveller, with any curiosity, will no doubt begin to wonder why so many villages in this part of the world were built in such apparently inaccessible spots. The reason of course was for their own self-defence, not against their neighbours, but against the frequent attacks of Algerian pirates. Whenever these corsairs could not find a ship to pillage, they would swoop down on the nearest coast, and kill or carry off the inhabitants of any village they were fortunate enough to surprise. Raids such as these were of frequent occurrence in this part of the country, all through the Middle Ages, and the natives do not appear to have been quite secure from them until well into the nineteenth century.

But although Peillon is 1600 feet above the sea, it is easily reached from the road in about half-an-hour. It is, however, rather a steep climb, and the view from the top disappointing, considering the extreme beauty of the scenery from below. From an artist's point of view, I know of no place for many miles round Monte Carlo that can be compared with Peillon for

Peille

picturesqueness, and one cannot help thinking what a superb picture Turner would have made of it.

After stopping for five minutes to admire the scenery, we continue along the road and turn to the left just beneath the village, and after pursuing this branch for about two and a half kilomètres, we arrive at the Buvette where we intend to lunch. This is called the 'Point de la Grave,' and is about fifteen kilomètres from the Monastery of Laghet. We can here obtain some native wine, and if necessary they would no doubt be glad to give you some boiled eggs or even an omelette, but it is better to bring some sandwiches, in case their supplies have run out.

After lunch we went for a short stroll and admired the fine view of the little village of Peille, which is situated above us to the northeast 2000 feet above the sea, but fully sheltered by the majestic Mount Baudon, which towers up behind it for at least another 2000 feet. The Pic de Baudon is the highest point for many miles round, and is nearly 400 feet higher than Mont Agel, the lofty peak immediately behind Monte Carlo.

From the Buvette to Nice is only about fifteen kilomètres, and being downhill all the way, can easily be ridden in about an hour. At

Ten Days at Monte Carlo

Nice we took an early train to Monte Carlo, and were in our places at the Casino soon after five.

The table ran as follows:

SEVENTH DAY'S PLAY.

Black.	Red.	Score.	Black.	Red.	Score.
	30	No Stake	28		−2
17		No Stake			1 L
11		St. 1 L			
26		1 W	13		−3
					1 W
	34	0			
		1 L	13		−2
					1 W
	32	−1			
		1 L	20		−1
					1 W
28		−2			
		1 L	10		0
					1 W
	5	−3			
		1 W			+1
13		−2		23	St. 1 L
		1 W	31		1 W
26		−1			
		1 L	24		0
					1 L
4		−2			
		1 W	24		−1
					1 W
	Z.	−1			
		1 L	22		0
					1 W
	25	−2			
		1 L			+1
29		−3			
		1 W			
		−2			

Seventh Day's Play

Black.	Red.	Score.	Black.	Red.	Score.
	12	1 L			− 3
	34	1 L		9	1 L
11		− 2			− 4
		1 L		1	1 L
	18	− 3			− 5
		1 W		9	1 W
	16	− 2	17		− 4
		1 L			1 L
	34	− 3	13		− 5
		1 W			1 L
	32	− 2		34	− 6
		1 W			1 L
35		− 1	Z.		− 7
		1 L			1 L
	23	− 2		27	− 8
		1 W			1 L
	12	− 1	22		− 9
		1 L			1 L
20		− 2		12	− 10
		1 L			St. 2 W
17		− 3		21	− 8
		1 L			2 L
	Z.	− 4		7	− 10
		1 L			2 W
26		− 5		3	− 8
		1 W			2 W
4		− 4		23	− 6
		1 W			2 W
		− 3			− 4

Ten Days at Monte Carlo

Black.	Red.	Score.	Black.	Red.	Score.
2		−4 2 L		5	−6 2 L
	5	−6 2 W		3	−8 2 W
	16	−4 2 L		14	−6 2 W
13		−6 2 L	8		−4 2 L
	19	−8 2 W		30	−6 2 W
31		−6 2 W	24		−4 2 W
35		−4 2 L		1	−2 2 W
2		−6 2 W	28		0 1 W
	21	−4 2 L			+1
		−6 c.			

Zero Fund.

Fcs. 50 on 10th coup.
  50 „ 35th „
  50 „ 44th „
Fcs. 150

Summary.

Coups played . . . 68
  Won 33
  Lost 35
Units won 3

3 units @ fcs. 100 = fcs. 300
Add Zero Fund . . 150
  Total won . 450

Dinner at 'The Grand'

We win our first unit on the 17th 'coup,' and another one on the 22nd. The table then begins to run against us, and zero comes up twice, so that on the 47th spin we have to double our unit. Our luck then improves, and in the next twenty 'coups' we once more bring the score level. We win the 69th 'coup,' which makes us three units to the good, and having now 150 francs to the credit of 'Zero Fund,' we are enabled to retire with 450 francs in hand. The *séance* lasted about an hour and a half. We then went over to the Grand Hotel, and ordered some dinner for eight o'clock.

The cooking at the Grand is, in the opinion of most connoisseurs, the best in Monte Carlo. The restaurant is, after the Paris, the largest in the place, and it is admirably managed. This is not to be wondered at when one considers that the chairman of the Company is the Hon. Algernon Bourke, who has achieved such great success in London, both at Willis's Rooms and White's Club, whilst amongst the directors are Messrs. Ritz and Échenard, late of the Savoy in London, and at the present moment engaged in organizing what promises to be the best hotel of its size in the world, viz. the Hôtel Ritz, in the Place Vendôme, Paris.

Mr. Ritz has the reputation of being the best organizer of hotels in Europe, and with Monsieur Échenard to manage the restaurant, and Monsieur Escoffier as *chef de cuisine*, his success in Paris is assured.

But to return to the restaurant of the Grand Hotel; if you wish to be well looked after, you must get hold of François. He it is who here corresponds to Ciro in his own restaurant, and to Fleury at the Paris. It is he who will allot you a table, and order you a dinner short or long, rich or plain, expensive or moderate in price, just as you may elect; he will tell you what wine and what brandy to drink; he will arrange your floral decorations, if there are ladies in your party; and when half-past eight arrives, he will tell you the names of all the celebrities in the room.

But you must not forget one thing, and that is, that whilst Fleury is manager at the Paris, François is here only *maître d'hôtel*, and as he is probably not paid at all by the Company, he is entirely dependent upon the generosity of the clients. You must therefore bring it home to him in an unmistakable manner that you desire his personal attention. Not only will you never have cause to regret it, but you will even save money in the long run by being generous. The fact of the matter is, that not one Englishman in a hundred knows how to order a dinner in a French restaurant, and he will often increase his bill 30 per cent. through ignorance of the customs of the place. I know a man who goes and stops at the Grand for about ten days every year. Being most hospitably inclined he usually has a dinner-party every other night. The first thing he does on arrival is to enlist François' services with a handsome *douceur*, and not only does he get more attention than any one in the restaurant, but he has probably saved the amount of his tip on the first two dinner-parties. As he very justly remarks: "Supposing we are a party of twelve, I should, if left to myself, probably order nine portions of soup, fish, and asparagus, whereas François orders me about five of each and makes them go round, and with asparagus alone at ten francs a portion, there is probably fifty francs saved on the first large party I give."

English people who have not travelled much do not realize the extent to which the *pourboire* system is carried on in France, and if they have cause to complain of the inattention or incivility of servants, it is entirely due to their own stinginess. As a matter of fact hardly any of the chambermaids, waiters, or porters at the hotels are paid at all, and at a restaurant like the Paris or the Grand at Monte Carlo, the waiters probably have to pay the hotel as much as ten francs a day for being allowed to wait at table. But so thoroughly is the system now recognized on the Continent, and also in the first-class places in London, that I have known waiters paying 7.50 francs and 10 francs per day, who were able to save 200 francs a month. The result is that where so much liberality prevails, the stingy people will be made to suffer.

The following is a very good scale on which to base your *pourboires*, and without being extravagant will assure you good attendance in any restaurant. On a bill of from one to 50 francs, 10 per cent. of the bill; from 50 francs to 500 francs, about $7\frac{1}{2}$ per cent.; and if over 500 francs, about 5 per cent. English people have the idea that a franc a head is the proper tip to give, and I have often seen rich Englishmen after a long dinner of five people at a restaurant like the Grand, where the bill probably came to about 180 francs, give the waiters 5 francs, when from a liberal customer they would have got as much as twelve. The consequence is, that the attention they receive diminishes every time they visit that particular restaurant.

People may well argue that to increase your tips in proportion to the amount of your bill is a very bad system, as it encourages the waiters to run up the total of your bill. I cannot deny that this seems logical, but can only repeat that

Distinguished Visitors

the system is recognized and followed by most people in first-class French restaurants, and this being so, if you attempt to fight against it, you will be sure to suffer from inattention.

Frank was much too old a hand not to be conversant with all these little details, and having secured the services of François, and left the ordering of the dinner to him, we were given a table in the first room, which is specially reserved for the best customers of the house. When the season is in full swing, the company in this particular room is always select, and is generally made up of some of the smartest people in London.

On the left, as we enter the room, Mr. and Mrs. William McEwan are entertaining the Duke of Cambridge and a party of friends. Next to them Miss Fleetwood Wilson is giving a small dinner to meet the Grand Duke Michael and the Countess Torby. The Prince of Wales is at another table with Lord and Lady St. Oswald, Sir Edward and Lady Colebrooke, Princess Henry of Pless, Miss Agnes Keyser, Lord Rowton, and Sir Arthur Sullivan.

Mr. Gordon Bennett and Mr. H. Cosmo Bonsor, M.P. are also dispensing lavish hospitality, while the Duke and Duchess of Marlborough may be seen dining *tête-à-tête* in a corner of the room. As all the tables are decorated with masses of roses and carnations, the sight is a particularly gay and animated one.

Watch François as he cuts up a Rouennais duck in the twinkling of an eye and pops the carcase into a press for the juice to be squeezed out! Artistic carving is cultivated at a place like this, and ducks, chicken, woodcock, saddles of lamb, and *entrecôtes* seem to come all alike to François. They are cut up and dispensed to their respective tables with the most astonishing rapidity. The following is the dinner we had, and is a very fair sample of what the Grand Hotel does best:

Hors d'Œuvre.
Petite Marmite.
Filets de Sole Walewska.
Noisettes de Mouton, Richelieu.
Bécassines en Casserole.
Salade.
Asperges d'Argenteuil, Sauce Mousseline.
Mandarines glacées.
Café.
Vin.—St. Marceaux, 1889, Vin Brut.
Liqueur.—Curaçoa Marnier, Cordon Rouge.

There are two dishes on the above *menu* which may be said to be specialities of the Grand, viz. the *Sole Walewska* and the *Mandarines glacées;* I recommend you to try them both. The St. Marceaux Brut of 1889

Dinner at 'The Grand'

is probably the best champagne in Monte Carlo, and the Curaçoa Marnier is a most delicious liqueur, but be sure you get the *Cordon Rouge*.

Our bill was as follows:

GRAND HOTEL, MONTE CARLO.

	fcs.	c.
2 Couverts	1	
St. Marceaux Brut, 1889	19	
Hors d'Œuvre	1	50
Marmite	4	
Sole Walewska	5	
Noisettes de Mouton	5	
Bécassines, Salade	8	
Asperges d'Argenteuil	12	
Mandarines glacées	3	
2 Cafés	2	
2 Verres Marnier, Cordon Rouge	4	
Total	64	50

CHAPTER XI

Seventh Ride—The Man who played successfully for Ten Years—Cagnes—Biot—Antibes—Juan-les-Pins—Cap d'Antibes—Eighth Day's Play—Hôtel Terminus at Nice.

HAVING now won every day for a week, we found that we were beginning to attract a certain amount of attention in Monte Carlo, and our system began to be discussed by the gossips at the Métropole. We had previously agreed to let no one into the secret of how much we won, or how we did it. If any one asked us how we were getting on, we simply told them that we were still winning, and the result was, that most exaggerated accounts of our doings were daily repeated.

There was one old Englishman in our hotel called W——, who was crazy on the subject of systems. He had spent his whole life in travelling about from one gambling resort to another, and being a most superstitious and

The Successful Player

excitable person and an extremely bad gambler, he found very little difficulty in losing about two-thirds of his income, playing at the different tables he visited.

He professed to have tried every system that was ever invented without succeeding in winning, and nothing annoyed him more than to be told that it was possible to win on a system. The fact of the matter was, that he had never given any system a fair chance, as he was much too excitable, and had very little capital. His usual game was to take five louis over to the Casino, but whatever luck he was in, he never used to bring anything back; sometimes he would lose all his capital in a very short time, but sometimes, when he was in luck, he would turn his five louis into £100. Whichever it was, it did not seem to make any difference, for he would invariably remain at the tables until the whole of the £100 was gone. His only chance of ever coming out a winner was to be overtaken by the clock, and turned out of the Rooms at closing time, before he had been able to lose back all his winnings. Unfortunately for him this was a very rare occurrence, as he generally started playing too early in the day.

When some one informed him that we were supposed to have an infallible system, and had won every day for a week, he was very scornful, and came to me with such an officious and patronizing kind of manner that I resolved to "take a rise out of him."

"Do you imagine," he said, "that you have really discovered a system that is any good?"

I told him that as far as we had tried it, we were very well satisfied with our experiments.

"Ah," he said, "you may perhaps have won for a day or two, by exceptionally good luck, but if you think it is going to last, you will very soon find out your mistake. You can't *really* suppose that it is possible to play here every day and make money?" This in his most compassionate tone of voice.

"It may seem very strange to you," I replied, "but I am foolish enough to believe in such a possibility."

"Then," he said, "you must be mad. Has it never struck you that if such a thing were possible, there would be hundreds of people here doing it? Now do you know *any one* who has done it, even every day for a year?" By this time quite a little crowd had collected round us in the hall of the Métropole, listening to the discussion.

"Yes," I said, "I do know a man who has played here every day of his life for the last ten years and made money all the time."

"Quite impossible, utterly impossible," said

The Successful Player

W——. "Why, such a thing has never been known since gambling was first invented!"

"Gambling," I replied quietly, "I said nothing about gambling; the man I am referring to plays the violin in the orchestra!"

Our excitable friend withdrew amid roars of laughter, and he never wished to discuss systems with me again after that day.

Our programme to-day was to have a ride of about forty-five kilomètres, which was rather more than our usual distance; but the road traversed is flat almost all the way, and as it follows the railway the rider can always take a train in the event of fatigue.

We take the 9.40 a.m train from Monte Carlo to Cagnes, which is twelve kilomètres the other side of Nice. On leaving the station we find ourselves on the Route Nationale from Nice to Cannes, and a good, broad, flat road it is, with a fair surface in good weather. We turn to the left and ride out of the village towards Cannes.

After going three kilomètres, we come to about as fine a piece of road for 'scorching' as the most fastidious of 'scorchers' can desire. It is dead flat for five kilomètres, perfectly straight, and with hardly any traffic except on Sundays, when you will find it well patronized by cyclists and motors. All can turn on full speed here, for it is perfectly safe, and there is no scenery to distract one. Six kilomètres after leaving Cagnes, we notice a road leading off to the right. This goes to Biot, an interesting little village built on a hill about four kilomètres from the Route Nationale. This would make a nice little excursion for any one who chose to ride out from Nice and back, but one would have to take sandwiches, as the restaurant at Biot is not to be depended upon except for native wine. The total distance from Nice to Biot and back is about forty-three kilomètres.

We continue on our way and soon come to Antibes, which is about ten kilomètres from Cagnes. The main road does not enter the town, but skirts it on the north side, and instead of turning to the left and entering the fortifications we continue along the road to Cannes down an avenue of trees. We then mount a stiffish incline of about 300 yards, cross a railway bridge, and see the station of Juan-les-Pins on our left. Here we cross the line at a level crossing and ask for the Grand Hotel, which is close to the station.

The rider can either lunch here, or can ride on another two kilomètres to the hotel at Cap d'Antibes. Both are good hotels, where they provide a very fair lunch at a moderate price; both have nice gardens in which to drink your coffee and smoke a cigar, but of the two views

Antibes

we preferred that from Juan-les-Pins, and we were lucky enough to find the French Mediterranean Squadron at anchor in the roadstead.

After lunch we rode round Cap d'Antibes, and into the little town from the south-west. If there is not much to be seen in the town itself, at any rate there is one of the finest views on the whole Riviera from just outside it.

You get the little harbour in the foreground, well filled with fishing-boats; beyond is the town and the picturesque old Fort, whilst the background is a magnificent range of snow mountains. This is by far the finest view of the Maritime Alps that can be obtained within easy reach of Monte Carlo, and late in the afternoon of a clear day it makes a really beautiful picture.

Antibes used to be considered a place of great strength, and was no doubt strongly fortified owing to its being until 1860 the last seaboard town in France. Both the breakwater and the old fortifications were constructed by the great engineer Vauban, and the old Fort must have been almost impregnable before the days of modern artillery. The town was bombarded and nearly demolished by the English Fleet on three different occasions.

The ride back from Antibes to Nice is about twenty-two kilomètres, and needs little description, as the ground has all been traversed on a former occasion. Just before entering Cagnes

Ten Days at Monte Carlo

we cross the river Loup, and get a fine view of the Castle of Villeneuve-Loubet, standing on a hill about two miles to our left.

We reach Nice in time to have some tea, and catch the five o'clock train to Monte Carlo. We commenced operations at the Casino soon after six, when the following numbers appeared:

EIGHTH DAY'S PLAY.

Black.	Red.	Score.	Black.	Red.	Score.
33	14	No Stake	20		− 5 1 L
	25	No Stake St. 1 W			
31	32	St. 1 L 1 L		27	− 6 1 W
6		− 2 1 L		27	− 5 1 L
	5	− 3 1 L		30	− 6 1 W
	9	− 4 1 L	22		− 5 1 L
29		− 5 1 L		23	− 6 1 W
	23	− 6 1 W	13		− 5 1 W
	1	− 5 1 L	2.		− 4 1 L
	25	− 6 1 W	4		− 5 1 L
		− 5			− 6

Eighth Day's Play

Black.	Red.	Score.	Black.	Red.	Score.
	16	− 6 1 L	Z.		− 6 1 L
	3	− 7 1 L		21	− 7 1 W
20		− 8 1 L		34	− 6 1 L
	25	− 9 1 W		16	− 7 1 W
24		− 8 1 W		12	− 6 1 W
	30	− 7 1 W		34	− 5 1 W
10		− 6 1 W		3	− 4 1 W
	21	− 5 1 W		16	− 3 1 W
	9	− 4 1 L		21	− 2 1 W
	3	− 5 1 W	22		− 1 1 L
35		− 4 1 L		3	− 2 1 W
10		− 5 1 L		36	− 1 1 L
	25	− 6 1 L	24		− 2 1 L
2		− 7 1 W		23	− 3 1 W
		− 6			− 2

Ten Days at Monte Carlo

Black.	Red.	Score.	Black.	Red.	Score.
11		− 2 1 W	35		0 1 W
	12	− 1 1 W			+ 1
		0		18	+ 1 W

<table>
<tr><td>

Zero Fund.

Fcs. 50 on 18th coup
<u> 50</u> ,, 34th ,,
Fcs. 100

</td><td>

Summary.

Coups played 51
Won .. 27
Lost .. 24
Units won . 3

3 units @ fcs. 100 = fcs. 300
Add Zero Fund . . 100
Total won . 400

</td></tr>
</table>

We win a unit on the very first 'coup,' and afterwards come in for an adverse run of six. A long struggle then takes place between the Bank and ourselves. We arrive at − 9 on two different occasions, but are never able to double the unit, as our luck always turns before − 10 is reached.

However, our patience is rewarded at last, and we eventually come in for eight Reds, and an unfinished run of seven intermittences. This enables us to win another two units, and as we have now 100 francs to the credit of 'Zero Fund,' we can leave off winners of 400 francs.

Hôtel Terminus, Nice

As we intended to take the first train on the following morning from Nice to Puget-Théniers, it was necessary for us to sleep at Nice. We accordingly had an early dinner at the Métropole, and took our bags and 'bikes' over to Nice by the 9.45 p.m. train.

We put up at the Terminus, which is one of the most comfortable and best managed hotels in the place, and it is most conveniently situated just opposite the railway-station. As we had to turn out the next morning at six, we went straight to bed on our arrival.

CHAPTER XII

Eighth Ride—Puget-Théniers—Entrevaux—Touet de Beuil—La Mescla—St. Martin du Var—Ninth Day's Play.

IN order to get to Puget-Théniers in time to visit Entrevaux and have a comfortable ride home, it is necessary to leave Nice by the 6.50 a.m. train.

The station of the Sud de la France railway is about three minutes' ride from the Hôtel Terminus, and is to the north of the P. L. M. line, about a quarter of a mile up the Avenue de la Gare. If you should make the trip on a Sunday or a *fête* day, it is advisable to arrive at the station in good time, as there is sure to be a crowd, and if you are late your bicycle may get left behind.

The railway leaves Nice to the north-west, up the pretty little valley of the Magnan, and after about a quarter of an hour we stop at the station of St. Isidore. Early May is the time to see

Nice to Puget-Théniers

this part of the line in all its beauty, with every hedge a rose-garden, and every field a mass of wild-flowers and poppies.

Soon after leaving St. Isidore, we emerge into the valley of the Var, and arrive at Colomars at 7.30. The view from Colomars station has already been described in Chapter VIII. Let us hope that you will be as lucky as we were, and have a perfectly clear day for your excursion, as the beauty of the scene is considerably diminished when the tops of the mountains are hidden in mist. A good volume of water in the river is also required to add to the grandeur.

We were extremely fortunate in both these respects, but were not so lucky as regards the wind. There was a good stiff breeze blowing right up the valley, which was quite sufficient to prevent us from 'coasting' at any part of the ride home. Unfortunately for cyclists, the wind has a tendency to blow up this valley, and I have experienced it so strong, that although the road descends the whole way to Colomars, in some places it seemed to us like hill climbing.

After leaving Colomars, instead of crossing the river and climbing the hill to Gattières, the train continues straight up the valley, and follows the river Var for the remainder of the journey. Picturesque little villages will be seen perched high on the mountains on each side of the line.

To the right La Roquette, and to the left Bonson, are the two most remarkable, the latter being built on the edge of a cliff rising sheer out of the valley to an altitude of over 1000 feet.

After leaving St. Martin du Var, the mountains close in, and the line runs for several kilomètres through a narrow gorge, in some places not more than sixty yards wide. At La Mescla the railway, which has hitherto been going due north, suddenly curves round to the left, and starts running in an almost westerly direction; and this course it pursues for the rest of the journey. Several tributaries flow into the Var, all the important ones coming from the east or north. The first of these is the river Vésubie, the next La Tinée, and then the pretty little torrent of Cians (famous for its trout), which joins the main stream fifty-five kilomètres from Nice.

At Touet de Beuil it is advisable to leave word at the station that you require lunch for your party at about mid-day. They will deliver your message at the Hôtel Latty, which is just opposite, and you will then find the *déjeuner* all ready on your arrival. Should your party consist of more than four, it would be better to send them a wire the day before, as no doubt supplies are sometimes rather limited in these out-of-the-way places. We arrive at Puget-Théniers at 9.35.

There is absolutely nothing of interest to be seen here, so we mount our machines and ride straight up the valley to Entrevaux. This is an almost flat ride of six kilomètres, and we found it particularly easy with the wind behind us all the way. And here let me warn you, that although we lay no claim to the distinction of having discovered the little town of Entrevaux, nevertheless its existence is completely ignored by nearly all the guide-books to the Riviera. This is all the more extraordinary when you come to consider that there are few more interesting places in the whole neighbourhood. Its curious situation, its picturesque old drawbridge, and its imposing-looking fortress, all make it well worth a visit.

The river Var here bends sharply round to the north, at something more than a right angle, and the town being built inside the curve made by the stream, it is surrounded on three sides by a roaring torrent. There is no access to it from behind, as it is built up the side of a mountain, the summit of which is crowned by an apparently impregnable fortress, commanding the valley to the east and west.

Owing to the great strength of its position, Entrevaux has been the scene of many a bloody encounter. It was taken by Charles V. in 1536, but the citadel was subsequently recaptured by the inhabitants and mountaineers, and given by them to Francis I., who granted them numerous privileges in return. Since that time it has always belonged to France, and it was probably the only town on the east side of the river that was French; as up to the year 1860, and before the annexation of Nice, the Var was the boundary between France and Italy.

It seems, that when attacked, the inhabitants used to raise the drawbridge and defend the approaches to the town, as long as possible, from the battlements below. If the enemy succeeded in crossing the river and making a breach in the walls, the defenders would then retire to the fortress on the hill, where they were no doubt able to hold out for many weeks, and make things very uncomfortable for the attacking party below. The only approach to the citadel is by a steep and narrow causeway, through a series of about twenty gateways, each of which in turn could doubtless have been held by a few brave men against an entire army.

Strangers have to get special permission to visit the fortress, and carriages are not allowed to cross the drawbridge owing to the narrowness of the streets of the town.

Touet de Beuil

Having thoroughly explored Entrevaux, we turn our faces homewards, and ride down the valley.

Puget-Théniers being a dirty and evil-smelling village, without apparently a single redeeming feature, we ride straight through it without dismounting.

The road, the river, and the railway run parallel to one another the whole way down to Colomars, and so good is the surface, and so continuous the gradual descent, that on a still day one can 'coast' with safety almost the entire distance from Puget-Théniers to St. Martin du Var.

About four miles down the road an enormous square-shaped mountain appears in front of us like a mighty fortress commanding the valley, and just beyond this we cross the river Cians and arrive at Touet de Beuil. The Hôtel Latty is down a road to the right, close to the railway-station. Here they will give you a very good lunch, considering the distance from civilization, and the native white wine is dry, and exceedingly palatable.

If you feel sufficiently energetic after lunch, you should certainly climb up and explore the little village of Touet de Beuil; the view from the church being very striking. The curious feature about the place is that the church is built on the top of a torrent, the waters of which run right underneath the edifice.

From Touet de Beuil to La Vésubie is perhaps the most interesting part of our ride, the scenery all round La Mescla being especially fine. So narrow is the gorge in places, that there is only just room for the road and the river, the railway having to tunnel through the solid rock. Occasionally even the road has to be taken through short tunnels. Just after crossing the bridge at La Mescla we notice a road branching off to the left: this runs right up the valley of La Tinée to a place called St. Sauveur, which is about the same distance from Nice as Puget-Théniers.

It all depends upon the wind and the condition of the rider how much further down the valley you will ride. By the time we reached La Vésubie we had done forty-seven kilomètres, and were still comparatively fresh. Had there been no wind we should have ridden down to Colomars, but as it was, we decided to ride only as far as St. Martin du Var, which gave us altogether a ride of about fifty-three kilomètres. Here we took the five o'clock train, which brought us to Nice soon after six.

As we did not reach Monte Carlo till seven o'clock, we decided that the best thing would be to have some tea and a couple of boiled eggs

Ninth Day's Play

before going to the Casino, seeing we were likely to find the rooms too crowded if we waited till after dinner. By these means we were able to start playing at eight o'clock, and were ensured a nice quiet hour at least before the crowd came in. It so happened that the table was in the best of humours, and we caught it running most favourably for our system. The following were the figures of the play:

NINTH DAY'S PLAY.

Black.	Red.	Score.	Black.	Red.	Score.
	12	No Stake			0
	5	No Stake		18	1 L
17		St. 1 L			−1
	Z.	1 L		25	1 W
29		−2 1 L	Z.		0 1 L
24		−3 1 W		7	−1 1 W
29		−2 1 W		9	0 1 W
	27	−1 1 L			+1
13		−2 1 W	31	7	1 L 1 W
	32	−1 1 W	Z.		0 1 L
		0			−1

Ten Days at Monte Carlo

Black.	Red.	Score.	Black.	Red.	Score.
	34	−1 1 L	8		0 1 W
26		−2 1 L			+1
	3	−3 1 W	33 33		1 L 1 W
8		−2 1 W	22		0 1 W
	18	−1 1 W			+1
		0	15		1 W

ZERO FUND.
Fcs. 50 on 2nd coup.
    50 ,, 11th ,,
    50 ,, 16th ,,
    150

SUMMARY.
Coups played . . 26
Won 15
Lost 11
Units won . . . 4

4 units @ fcs. 100 = fcs. 400
Add Zero Fund . . 150
Total won . 550

We win our first unit on the 13th 'coup,' and have already got 100 francs to the credit of 'Zero Fund.'

In spite of another zero we win our second unit on the 22nd spin. We then find that we are on a run of five Blacks, and are able to retire on the 26th 'coup,' the winners of four units, plus 150 francs to the credit of 'Zero Fund.'

Supper at Ciro's

As it was still quite early we went into the concert, which lasted till ten, and afterwards went over to Ciro's and had a nice light little supper, consisting of some devilled kidneys and a couple of snipe on toast, washed down with a bottle of Pommery. We then retired to the smoking-room of the Métropole for cigars, after which we felt quite ready for bed.

CHAPTER XIII

Ninth Ride—Laghet—Contes—Nice - Riquier—Tenth Day's Play—Summary of Ten Days' Results—Total Expenses and Net Profit.

As the expedition to Entrevaux had given us rather a long day, we decided that our last ride should be a fairly short and easy one, enabling us to get back in good time to Monte Carlo. Frank accordingly proposed to take me up a hitherto unexplored valley to a little village called Contes.

We started off by train to La Turbie, and thence *viâ* Laghet to Trinité Victor, exactly as described on page 86. After passing through Drap, instead of turning off to the right, up the valley of the Paillon to Peille, we keep straight along the main road for about another kilomètre. We then see a road branching off to the left, and it is this that leads to Contes.

The main road, which we leave at this point,

continues to Escarène and over the Col de Braus to Sospel, from whence there is a very good road leading down to Mentone; but this is a ride which should only be undertaken by athletes, for the hills are tremendous, and in one place the road runs up to an altitude of over 3000 feet. The distance by this route from Nice to Mentone is about sixty-five kilomètres, but it is equal to over 100 on the flat.

The branch road leading to Contes is rather cut up in places, and requires careful riding, but the distance from the Route Nationale to the village is only about four kilomètres. We pass some hideous-looking cement works, and notice a road leading off to the right. This goes to La Vernea and Sclos, and would make a nice excursion for another day, if we had time; the road, however, is bad and even dangerous in places.

And now we see the little town of Contes about a mile off, built in terraces up the side of a mountain at the end of the valley. Contes is peaceful and homely in appearance, and gives one the idea of more prosperity than most of the neighbouring villages. The pretty little church in the centre, with its red spire, makes it wonderfully picturesque.

The town is over 1200 feet above the sea, but is so surrounded by mountains, protecting it from every cold wind, that the olive, vine, and orange tree all thrive there equally well, and indeed this little valley is especially famous both for its olives and wine.

We see a restaurant straight in front of us, at the entrance to the town, and here we stop for lunch. The cooking was of the most primitive order, and I should recommend people who are at all fastidious to bring some sandwiches with them. The boiled eggs came up as if they had been reposing in lukewarm water for about a minute and a half, and the veal cutlets which followed were also half raw. Possibly fuel is costly in these parts! There was no fault, however, to be found with the white wine, which we found unusually refreshing. After lunch we climbed up the hill and had a look round the old village, but there is not very much of interest to be found there, with the exception of the church.

We then mounted our machines and rode straight down the valley to Nice, a distance of about sixteen kilomètres, downhill all the way. We took the train to Monte Carlo from Nice-Riquier, which is rather nearer than Nice station for any one coming down the Paillon valley. On our arrival we had some tea, and went over to the Casino soon after five o'clock.

The Bank was evidently determined to make

Tenth Day's Play

one last effort to clean us out before our departure, and at one time they had actually won back nearly all our winnings for the last nine days. After this they could do no more, and we slowly but surely made up our lost ground, and were able to leave them utterly defeated on the 62nd 'coup.'

TENTH DAY'S PLAY.

Black.	Red.	Score.	Black.	Red.	Score.
15 6		No Stake No Stake		7	−3 1 L
	30 16	St. 1 L 1 L	13		−4 1 L
	3	−2 1 W	29		−5 1 L
4		−1 1 L	2		−6 1 W
	27	−2 1 W		14	−5 1 L
28		−1 1 W		21	−6 1 L
	19	0 1 W		34	−7 1 W
		+1	24		−6 1 L
26		+1 W	33		−7 1 L
10	Z.	1 L 1 L			−8
	36	−2 1 L			
		−3			

[157]

Ten Days at Monte Carlo

Black.	Red.	Score.	Black.	Red.	Score.
	7	−8 1 L		27	−22 2 W
	12	−9 1 L		3	−20 2 L
22		−10 St. 2 L	8		−22 2 L
31		−12 2 L	11		−24 2 L
20		−14 2 W	17		−26 2 W
	9	−12 2 L		16	−24 2 L
	18	−14 2 L		21	−26 2 L
35		−16 2 L	31		−28 2 L
10		−18 2 L	4		−30 St. 3 L
	30	−20 2 L	Z.		−33 3 L
	23	−22 2 L	29		−36 3 W
	1	−24 2 W	6		−33 3 W
	14	−22 2 W		30	−30 3 L
29		−20 2 L	15		−33 3 W
		−22			−30

Hôtel Terminus, Nice

Black.	Red.	Score.	Black.	Red.	Score.
	1	−30 3 W		32	−15 3 W
8		−27 3 W		14	−12 3 W
	27	−24 3 W		25	−9 3 W
29		−21 3 W		18	−6 3 W
	23	−18 3 W	4		−3 3 L
	19	−15 3 L		5	−6 3 W
	12	−18 3 W	13		−3 3 W
		−15			0

ZERO FUND.
Fcs. 50 on 9th coup.
 150 ,, 44th ,,
Fcs. 200

SUMMARY.
Coups played 62
 Won 27
 Lost 35
Units won 2

2 units @ fcs. 100 = fcs. 200
Add Zero Fund . . 200
 Total won . 400

The table runs fairly well at the commencement, and we win our first unit on the 7th 'coup,' and another on the 8th. We then experience six consecutive losses, and four more shortly afterwards, which compels us to double our unit on the 23rd 'coup.' The table still continues to run very badly for us, and we encounter 'séries' of six, three, and five consecutive losing 'coups'; this forces us to treble our unit on the 43rd spin, and on the 45th 'coup' we are as much as 3600 francs to the bad.

The Bank, however, has now played itself entirely out, and it is our turn to have some luck. We come across six intermittences, and then a run of seven on the Red, and by the 62nd 'coup' we have made the score level. This enables us to retire, as we have won two units, and have now got 200 francs to the credit of 'Zero Fund.'

Having concluded our transactions with the Casino, and booked our places in the Train de Luxe for England, on the following day, we decided to celebrate our triumph by giving a small dinner-party at Ciro's restaurant. Blundell was of course invited, and one or two people to whom he had introduced us during our stay in Monte Carlo. Altogether we made up a very cheery little party of eight, and were fortunate enough to find Monsieur Ciro in quite his best form.

Next morning we amused ourselves by compiling a Summary of our ten days' operations at

Summary of Ten Days' Play

the Roulette Table. We found the result had been as follows:

Coups played	495
Won	242
Lost	253
Units won	29

29 Units @ fcs. 100	fcs. 2900
Add Zero Fund	1450
Total won	4350

Not such a bad result, considering that the Bank had won eleven more 'coups' than ourselves.

We then made a rough estimate of our expenses for the trip, which came to just about 3000 francs, as shown below:

Two First Return Tickets, abt.	fcs. 600
Two Train de Luxe Return Supplements, abt.	500
Excess luggage	200
Living expenses (ten days)	1500
Extras, tips, etc.	200
Total fcs.	3000

There accordingly remained the sum of about 1350 francs to be divided between us as net profit.

CHAPTER XIV

The Hotels and Restaurants of Monte Carlo—Monte Carlo Sharps and Swindlers—Hints to Visitors.

As regards hotels at Monte Carlo there is plenty of choice. The three best at present are the Métropole, the Grand, and the Hôtel de Paris, but in 1899 another will have to be added to this list, viz. the Riviera Palace Hotel at Bordina.

People who have not travelled much, and who do not speak French, will probably prefer the Métropole. Being one of the Gordon Hotels, it is of course thoroughly English in every respect. The architect was an Englishman, the furniture is by Maple and Co., and the bath-rooms and sanitary arrangements by Jennings. The situation is unique, being built on the side of a hill overlooking the Casino Gardens, with a beautiful view across the Bay of Roquebrune extending to Bordighera.

The Grand Hotel now also belongs to an English company, and though the public reception-rooms and the situation are not quite equal to the Métropole, the reputation of the cuisine is second to none. These two establishments usually open on December 1, and close about April 30.

The Hôtel de Paris, on the other hand, is open all the year round, and is one of the most cosmopolitan hotels in the world. English people are welcomed and made thoroughly comfortable, but it will be found that the foreign element usually predominates. The restaurant is essentially Parisian, and the wine-cellar the best on the Riviera. The Paris has the advantage of being the nearest hotel to the Casino.

These three establishments are all expensive, and their prices will be found to be about on a par.

After these come several first-class hotels, rather smaller, more unpretentious, and less expensive.

The Hôtel Victoria and the Prince de Galles belong to the Swiss firm of Rey Frères, and are as scrupulously clean and well-managed as most Swiss establishments.

The *clientèle* of the Hôtel Windsor is almost exclusively English, and this hotel can be confidently recommended, the food being excellent and the charges moderate.

Other hotels of the same class are the Hôtel Royal, the St. James's, the Hôtel Monte Carlo, and the Hôtel Helder. The latter is a new establishment situated just above the Métropole, and has already established a reputation for good cooking.

People who require cheaper accommodation should try the Hôtel de l'Europe, which is just below the Métropole and close to the railway-station. This belongs to François Rinjoux, the *maitre d'hôtel* of the Grand, and manager of the restaurant of the Hôtel Cecil in summer months. He gives you an excellent lunch or dinner for three francs or four francs respectively, wine being included, and he would probably take you *en pension* at very moderate rates. François possesses some of the best wine in Monte Carlo, his old Burgundies being especially good.

The Hôtel Savoy should also be mentioned for good cooking and good wine, but the charges are rather higher than at the Europe.

People requiring an *à la carte* restaurant, where they will not be overcharged, should try Ré's bar behind the English chemist, or the Princess's Restaurant, a new establishment, the proprietor of which has had experience in London, both at the Criterion and Tivoli.

Pension Arrangements

Should you intend only stopping a short time in Monte Carlo it will not be worth while to make '*pension* arrangements.' If you are making daily excursions, as we were, you will be paying for a lunch you will never eat; besides, you are sure to wish to dine out once or twice a week. Most of the hotels threaten to charge more for the rooms, if you take meals outside, but it is a threat that is seldom put into force.

It would seem almost unnecessary to warn people to be most careful about making acquaintances, either at the tables, in the hotels, or in railway travelling on the Riviera. During four months of the year this part of the world seems to be the happy hunting-ground of the cleverest and most refined scoundrels of Europe.

On the occasion of my first visit to Monte Carlo, I was dining alone one evening, when at the end of dinner a man, who had been sitting at a table close by, crossed over, and addressing me by name, reminded me that we had met some time ago at a London club in company of a certain Mr. W——. He said his name was Elwes. Now I knew Mr. W—— quite well, and remembered the name of Elwes, but could not for the life of me recollect if we had really met or not.

He asked me to dine with him the following evening, but as he seemed rather inclined to be over friendly, and as there was a something in his manner which I did not quite like, I made some excuse and got out of it. Whenever he saw me for the next day or two he was always trying to improve our acquaintance, but I noticed that he did not seem to have any other friends in the hotel.

A few days later the English detective attached to the Casino came and asked me if I knew a man called Elwes. I told him the story of our acquaintance, and inquired if *he* knew anything of him. He smiled grimly, and said: "Never you mind *what* I know, but I know quite enough to be sure he is after no good down here, and so told the Casino authorities to refuse him admission, and he then gave *your* name as a reference.

"I don't mind telling you," he added, "that his real name is not Elwes, and you probably have never met him before in your life."

After this, of course I took every opportunity of showing Mr. Elwes that I did not care for his society, and shortly afterwards he disappeared.

The detective would never tell me anything more about him that year, but the following season, about nine months afterwards, seeing me outside the Casino one day, he said: "By the way, I think I've got a newspaper cutting in my pocket-book which will interest you: read this."

And it certainly was interesting, for it was to the effect that John Ellison, *alias* Elwes, *alias* Grant (not to mention a few other *aliases*), had been sentenced at the Old Bailey to seven years' penal servitude for bank fraud.

The detective then told me that Elwes had been for some time the chief of a notorious gang of swindlers, and that they had come down to Monte Carlo the year before, with a big scheme to defraud the Casino. The whole business had been nipped in the bud, by Elwes being refused admission.

I well remember another and similar case. A well-dressed and gentlemanly little man, calling himself Dr. Pickering, was always trying to make acquaintances at the gambling-tables. He was very clever at it, for he would watch to see who your friends in the place were, and find out as much about them as possible.

Having acquired a certain amount of information about you, he would come and sit next to you at the tables for several days in succession, and make himself extremely pleasant, and talk of several of your friends as if he knew them quite well. As a matter of fact, he had only scraped their acquaintance in the same way as your own, by making out to them that he knew you.

In my own case he found out that a cousin

of mine went in for pony-racing, and commenced by informing me that my cousin Guy and he were great friends, "and saw a lot of one another pony-racing, don't you know." By these means, in about a month's time he had got to know a great number of people, including many ladies, and naturally the new-comers, seeing him talking to people they knew in 'the Rooms,' thought that he was 'all right.' So, in fact, did most of us until we heard one morning that a young Englishman had been drugged the night before, and relieved of 30,000 francs in hard cash at 'poker,' and that Dr. Pickering and two of his friends had left the place in a hurry.

Of course when I asked my cousin about him, on my return to England, he could not remember ever having met the man, any more than Mr. W—— could remember Elwes.

Beware of people who are extra polite and anxious to assist you at the tables. A friend of mine had an unpleasant experience. He could not get a seat at the Trente et Quarante, so had to stand and reach over the people's heads every time he wished to make a stake, or take off his winnings. He was playing in stakes of five louis, and sitting just in front of him was an extremely nice-looking, well-dressed French lady, who offered to hand up his money whenever he won, to save him the trouble of reaching over. He was of course very much obliged to her, and as she seemed to bring him luck, he stayed for half-an-hour or so at the same place, and won quite a nice little sum. It was only towards the end of his run that he thought the Bank had paid him one louis short on a certain winning stake, and when he found that he was certainly paid a louis too little on the next one he began to make a row. In the midst of the discussion with the croupier, the lady got up, saying something about " cette table m'apporte la guigne," and offered him her chair. The next day he met a friend who had had precisely the same experience, and they are now quite convinced that the lady had some cobbler's wax in the palm of her right glove, to which one louis adhered out of every little pile she handed up.

Talking of cobbler's wax reminds me of a very clever swindle perpetrated about two years ago on a Monte Carlo jeweller. A distinguished-looking gentleman came into the shop, and wished to look at some valuable diamond rings. Several trays were brought out and their contents examined, when suddenly the jeweller missed a ring worth about £400. He at once accused the customer of stealing it, but the latter was most indignant, and expressed himself as perfectly willing to be searched on the premises by the police.

So the police were sent for, and he was taken into a private room and thoroughly searched, but of course no ring was discovered, and the unfortunate jeweller was obliged to bow the gentleman out of his establishment with the most profuse apologies.

A short time afterwards a lady came into the shop and made some trifling purchase and went out again. The next morning, in dusting out the place, a piece of cobbler's wax was found underneath the counter, with the impression of the ring on it. The man had slipped the ring on to it whilst the jeweller's back was turned, and the lady, his accomplice, had doubtless removed it in the same way.

Beware of the man who has the reputation, either of being extraordinarily lucky, or of possessing an infallible system. There are several of these gentry, who have been hovering about the tables for years, and amongst them, I regret to say, one or two Englishmen. They encourage the idea that they always win in the long run, and endeavour to get unsuspecting people, generally youthful Englishmen, to gamble in partnership with them. Each is supposed to put in an equal amount of capital, and they start playing on a system together.

It is 'all on the square' at the commencement, and possibly you win a little the first day or two;

The Partnership Swindle

but one afternoon your partner will say to you at the tables, "It's beastly stuffy in here now; let's knock off for the present, and meet again after dinner, say about nine." He probably knows you are dining out, and are not likely to arrive till 9.15 or 9.30. You say "All right," and *he* takes charge of the capital.

In the evening you arrive at about ten minutes past nine, and find him sitting at the table, with a very long face. He says, "I'm awfully sorry, old chap; I got here rather before nine, but as the table seemed to be going well, and as I thought you would be sure to arrive in a few minutes, I started playing alone. We've had one of the worst runs I've ever seen, and they've been and cleaned us out."

He then shows you a card, marked with the numbers that are supposed to have come out, and of course you can say nothing. Next day he will probably tell you that such luck as you had on the day before does not occur more than once in six months, and will try and persuade you to provide new capital to get your losses back. But it is usually a case of 'once bit, twice shy,' and few are caught a second time.

I knew a case where the same man played this trick successfully on no less than three different young men, within the space of a fortnight, and must have netted at least £500.

He was a gentleman by birth, and very well connected, but so unscrupulous that I have no doubt whatever that he simply pocketed the money.

I knew another and still more extraordinary case, of a tall good-looking young Englishman, called Krugh, who had most charming manners, and always sported the colours of a well-known London Club. He was dressed quietly and in the best of taste, and quite devoid of any flashiness or swagger. He had been to a good public school, and soon made a great number of friends in Monte Carlo and the neighbourhood. He was very much in request at picnics during the day, and cotillon parties at night.

Krugh used to go in for unadulterated, barefaced robbery, without any redeeming features, and as he was content with very small amounts, and usually victimized unsuspecting ladies, he carried it on undiscovered for about four months.

He used to practise the partnership swindle to a great extent, but was quite satisfied to rob you of five or ten louis at a time. When ladies were confiding enough to let him hold their purses, he would deliberately steal as much as he thought would pass unnoticed.

But one fine day the bubble burst. A man named R—— arrived in Monte Carlo, who had once been Krugh's best friend. It then transpired that not only had Krugh been unable to resist stealing R——'s money and jewellery, but had robbed several of R——'s friends as well. A meeting of the victims took place in London, and they went in a body and informed Krugh that they intended to expose him. He went down on his knees and confessed the whole business, but begged so hard for mercy that they decided to let him off, provided he would resign from his Club and leave England.

As soon as R—— heard that Krugh was still wearing the Club colours, he of course told all the people he knew in Monte Carlo about the whole business, and in about two days' time Krugh slunk off, and went to America. I have since heard that he was carrying on the same little game over there, and after robbing many people who had been most kind to him, he was given twenty-four hours in which to leave New York or go to prison.

If you are playing on an even chance or a dozen, and leaving your winnings on the table to accumulate, it is as well to touch your pile with the rake, after every winning 'coup.' There is a sort of unwritten law, or at any rate etiquette, that if you touch a pile with the rake before the 'coup' is played, and no one objects to your doing so, it establishes your claim to it.

There are plenty of sharpers on the look-out for beginners, who do not know this custom, and after touching your pile (sometimes as if by accident), they will then put in a claim for it.

Should you have any money stolen, object at once and ask the croupier to pay you; if he should hesitate, leave your place and ask the 'Chef de Partie' to order him to pay you, and say that if he does not do so at once, you will appeal to the 'Directeur du Jour.' He will then usually pay you, but if he does not, make him send for the Director, and insist. Be very determined to get your money, but make as little noise as possible. They will almost always pay an Englishman, provided he insists and does not make a scene.

INDEX

ADMINISTRATION of Casino, 32, 33
Algerian Pirates, 122
Antibes, 138, 139
Augustan Monument, 79
'Avant Dernier,' 20

BEAULIEU, 56, 72, 73
Bercy Sauce, 103
Bicycles, 29
Biot, 138
Blackmail, 35—37
Bonson, 146
Bordighera, 55
Bordina, 54
Boucher, 109
Bouillabaisse, 88
Bourke, Hon. A., 127
Bristol Hotel, 69, 88

CAB Fares, 180, 181
Cabbé Roquebrune, 120
Cagnes, 96, 114, 137—140
Cannes, 96, 105, 107, 137
Cap d'Ail, 68
Cap d'Antibes, 138, 139
Cap Martin, 42, 53, 58, 59
Cap Martin Hotel, 57, 58
Cap St. Hospice, 87
Casino Customs, 32—37, 173
Cemetery, 67
Champagne St. Marceaux, 132
Château Carbonnieux, 49
Cimiez, 70
Ciro and Ciro's Restaurant, 43—48, 160

Climate of Monte Carlo, 41
Col de Braus, 155
Colomars, 94, 105, 150
Concerts, 74
Condamine, 65
Consul, English, 179
Contes, 154—156
Corniche Road, 57, 58
Corsanego, Monsieur, 77
Crémaillère, 53, 79, 119
Curaçoa Marnier, 133
Custom House, 38

DEMI-MONDE, 102
Dentist, English, 179
Doctors, English, 179
Drap, 121, 154

EDEN Hotel, 68
Emperor of Austria, 59
Empress Eugénie, 58
Entrevaux, 105, 143—150
Escarène, 155
Esterels, 56, 70
Expenses of Trip, 161
'Ex Votos,' 81, 86
Eze, 55, 56, 69, 72

FLEURY, Monsieur, 101—104
Fragonard, 106—112
François, 128—133, 164
French, mistakes in, 97—100

GATTIÈRES, 95, 145
Gorbio, 120
Gordon Hotels, 162

Index

Gorges du Loup, 105, 113
Grand Hotel, Grasse, 107, 113
Grand Hotel, Juan-les-Pins, 138
Grand Hotel, Monte Carlo, 127—133, 163
Grasse, 94, 105—114
Gratuities, scale of, 129—131

HOTELS of Monte Carlo, 162—165

INTERNATIONAL Sleeping Car Company, 37, 54

JEHIN, Léon, 74
Jerry Thomas, 46
Journey to Monte Carlo, 38
Juan-les-Pins, 138, 139

KILOMÈTRES, 55

LAGHET, 80—86, 119, 120
La Mescla, 146, 150
La Roquette, 146
La Tinée, 146, 150
La Turbie, 53, 73, 79, 120
La Vernea, 155
La Vésubie, 146, 150
Latty Hotel, 146, 149
Le Var, 93, 94, 145—150
London House, 71
Loup, River, 114

MAGAGNOSC, 113
Magnan Valley, 144
Mails, 180
Malet, Sir Edward, 67, 69
Mulvilan, Monsieur, 106—112
Maple, Sir J. B., 69
Maps of Riviera, 28
Maritime Alps, 139
Martello Tower, 88
May, beauties of, 42, 144
McCalmont, Mr. H., 69, 87
Mentone, 58, 120, 155
Métropole Hotel, 41, 162

Mistral, 41
Mont Agel, 120
Mont Boron, 70, 72
Mostèle, 49

NICE, 56, 65, 70, 71, 87

ORCHESTRA of Casino, 74—77

PAGANINI, 88
Paillon River, 57, 86, 93, 121
P. L. M. Railway, 78, 105
Paris, Hôtel de, 100—104, 163
Peille, 120, 123
Peillon, 119, 123
Pic de Baudon, 123
'Plaques,' 18, 99
Point de la Grave, 123
Pourboires, scale of, 129—131, 181
Press, 33, 36
Prince of Wales, 58, 131
Promenade des Anglais, 71, 94
Puget-Théniers, 93, 94, 143—150

RÉGENCE, Restaurant de la, 71, 87
Regina Palace, 70
Riquier, 156
Ritz, Mr., 127
Riviera Palace, Bordina, 162
Riviera Palace, Nice, 54
Roquebrune, 42, 54, 58
Rothschild, Baroness de, 113

SAINTE DÉVOTE, 65—67
St. Isidore, 144, 145
St. Jean, 56, 87
St. Jeannet, 95
St. Martin du Var, 146, 150
St. Paul, 96
St. Sauveur, 150
Salisbury, Lord, 69, 99
Sclos, 155
Sirocco, 42

Index

Smith, Edward, 58
Smith's Bank, 31, 33, 106, 107
Soufflé Surprise, 103
Sud de la France Railway, 93, 144—150
Summary of Play, 160, 161
Swindlers, etc., 165—174
Systems, 18

TELEGRAPHIC Rates, 176
Terminus Hotel, Nice, 143
Tête de Chien, 56, 58
Touet de Beuil, 146, 149, 150
Tourettes, 94, 95, 113
Touring Club de France, 27, 78

Train de Luxe, 37, 160
Trinité Victor, 57, 86, 121

ULRICH, Mr., 59

VARNIER, Monsieur, 42
Vence, 95
'Viatique,' 33
Villefranche, 69, 72, 87
Villeneuve-Loubet, 114, 140

WERTHEIMER, Charles, 47, 111

'ZERO Fund,' 15, 16

ADDENDA

ENGLISH DOCTORS AT MONTE CARLO

Dr. FAGGE, Villa de la Porte Rouge.
„ FITZGERALD, Villa Ciro.
„ PRYCE MITCHELL, Villa Henri.
„ ROLLA ROUSE, Winter Palace.
„ BARNARD, Villa Mai.

ENGLISH DENTIST

C. ASH, Esq., Villa Paola.

ENGLISH VICE-CONSUL

J. W. KEOGH, Esq., Villa Richemont.

ENGLISH BANK

Messrs. SMITH & Co., Chartered Bankers, Galerie Charles III.

Addenda

MAILS

Mails leave Monte Carlo for Paris and London, 1.40 p.m., 2.55 p.m., 7.45 p.m., and 11.30 p.m.

Mails leave Monte Carlo for Italy, etc., 6.45 a.m., and 9.55 p.m.

Mails arrive from Paris and London, 9 a.m., and 4.30 p.m.

Mails arrive from Italy, etc., 9 a.m., and 4.30 p.m.

TELEGRAPHIC RATES FROM MONACO

	Centimes
To France, Corsica, Algiers, Tunis, per word	5
„ Switzerland and Belgium	12.5
„ Germany	15
„ British Isles, Austria, Spain, Italy and Portugal	20
„ Gibraltar and Denmark	24.5
„ Malta and Russia	40
„ Greece	53.5

MONACO CAB FARES

IN THE PRINCIPALITY

From 7 a.m. till 12.30 p.m.

	Francs
The course	1.50
„ hour	3.00

From 12.30 p.m. till 7 a.m.

„ course	2.50
„ hour	5.00

Addenda

SPECIAL FARES

TO THE ENGLISH CHURCH

	Francs
By the course	2
„ „ hour	3
To Eze station and back with 1 hr. wait	8
„ Beaulieu and back with 1½ hrs. wait	13
„ Villefranche and back with 1½ hrs. wait	16
„ Nice and back with 3 hrs. wait	25
„ „ going or returning by Corniche road	40
„ Roquebrune station and back without waiting	5
„ Cap Martin Hotel and back with 1½ hrs. wait	10
„ Mentone and back with 1½ hrs. wait	14
„ Mentone *viâ* Cap Martin and back with 1½ hrs. wait	14
„ Roquebrune village and back with 1 hr. wait	12
„ La Turbie village and back with 1½ hrs. wait	18
„ Laghet village and back with 3 hrs. wait	25

If kept beyond the times specified, payment to be made at the rate of 3 francs per hour.

N.B.—Cabmen expect a *pourboire* in addition to the above fares at the rate of about 10 per cent. of the fare.

Richard Clay & Sons, Limited,
London & Bungay.

SMITH & CO.
BANKERS
Galerie Charles III, MONTE CARLO.

AGENTS FOR
The International Sleeping-Car Company
London, Chatham & Dover Railway Company
North German Lloyd
Hamburg American Steam Packet Company, etc.

TICKETS ISSUED
STEAMSHIP PASSAGES BOOKED
SLEEPING BERTHS SECURED
LONDON AGENTS: Lloyd's Bank, St. James's St.

See page 31.

LA LIQVOR
GRAND MARNIER

As supplied to
H.M. Queen Victoria; H.R.H. the Prince of Wales;
H.I.M. the Emperor of Austria; and to the
Court of Russia.

The best, purest and most digestive of liqueurs
Has a most exquisite orange flavour.

See page 132.

MONTE CARLO

Hôtel Métropole

Recently enlarged. Opens end of November. Occupies a beautiful position overlooking the sea and Public Gardens. It contains every possible comfort and luxury. Electric light throughout. Restaurant Français. Cuisine and Wines of the highest class. The Métropole Orchestra plays a selection of choice music during Luncheon and Dinner, and in Entrance Hall (4.30 to 5.30), throughout the Season. Lifts to all floors. Numerous Family Apartments with Bath-room, etc. Large number of Double and Single Bedrooms, all most comfortably furnished. Large Hall and Public Rooms. Perfect Sanitation.

Métropole Villas

Facing full South, communicate directly with the Hotel by covered corridor. All principal apartments have Private Bath-room, etc., and they therefore offer to Families all the quietude of a Private Residence with the convenience of a well-appointed Hotel.

Tariffs in London at the Grand, Métropole, or Victoria Hotels, and Brighton at the Hôtel Métropole.

CANNES
THE HÔTEL MÉTROPOLE
OPENS END OF OCTOBER.

Most beautifully situated in elevated and well-sheltered position, facing due South, twenty-seven acres of Garden and Pine Woods belonging to Hotel, including large Lawn Tennis Courts.

Numerous Family Apartments, with Bath-rooms, etc. Also large number of double and single Bedrooms, most comfortably furnished, all at very moderate prices. Lifts to all floors. Large Hall and Public Rooms. Electric Light everywhere. Perfect Sanitation by leading London Engineer. A most comfortable Hotel to pass the winter at.

TARIFFS, &c., in London at the GRAND, MÉTROPOLE, or VICTORIA HOTELS; and Brighton, at the MÉTROPOLE.

The Gordon Hotels

ARE

GRAND HOTEL	. LONDON.
HOTEL MÉTROPOLE and WHITEHALL ROOMS }	. LONDON.
HÔTEL VICTORIA .	. LONDON.
FIRST AVENUE HOTEL	. LONDON.
HÔTEL MÉTROPOLE and CLARENCE ROOMS }	. BRIGHTON.
BURLINGTON HOTEL .	. EASTBOURNE.
ROYAL PIER HOTEL .	. RYDE, I. of W.
CLIFTONVILLE HOTEL	. MARGATE.
LORD WARDEN HOTEL	. DOVER.
HÔTEL MÉTROPOLE .	. FOLKESTONE.
GRAND HOTEL . .	. BROADSTAIRS.

THE
INTERNATIONAL SLEEPING CAR CO.

Frequent Trains-de-Luxe to and from the Riviera. Sleeping Cars attached to all Rapide Trains.

London Office	14 Cockspur Street.
Paris	3 Place de l'Opera.
Monte Carlo	Gallery of the Grand Hotel and SMITH'S BANK.

The Official Guide and Time-Book of the Company, "THE CONTINENTAL TRAVELLER," sent post free on application.
See page 37.

MONTE CARLO
AND
TURBIE RAILWAY

Frequent Trains by this Mountain Railway to La Turbie (in 20 minutes), from whence a Magnificent View is obtained.

See pages 53, 78, etc.

THE
INTERNATIONAL PALACE CO.

(CIE. INTLE. DES GRANDS HOTELS)

The following is a list of the Company's Hotels—

The Riviera Palace	Monte Carlo
The Riviera Palace	Nice (Cimiez)
The Ghezireh Palace	Cairo
Shepheard's Hotel	Cairo
Elysée Palace Hotel	Paris
The Royal Château d'Ardennes	Ardennes
Pavilion de Bellevue	Paris (Meudon)
Hôtel Victoria	Ismailia
The Bosphorus Summer Palace	Therapia
The Hôtel de la Plage	Ostend
The Avenida Palace	Lisbon
The Pera Palace	Constantinople
The Grand Hotel International	Brindisi
Hôtel Stephanie, Casinos and Villas,	Abazzia (Istria)
The Hôtel Terminus (St. Jean)	Bordeaux

For Particulars apply to the Company's Offices,

**14, Cockspur Street, LONDON, S.W.
and 3, Place de l'Opera, PARIS.**

The Official Guide and Time-Book of the Company, "*THE CONTINENTAL TRAVELLER,*" *sent post free on application.*

See page 54.

SAVOY HOTEL

LONDON

OVERLOOKING RIVER AND EMBANKMENT GARDENS.

By day the most beautiful garden and river view in Europe. By night a fairy scene.

All charges for Rooms include Baths, Lights and Attendance.

Suites of rooms, Sitting, Bedroom, private Bath-room, etc., from 30/- a day. Single Bedrooms from 7/6. Double from 12/-. Special Telephone to Paris.

Every sitting-room suite has a private Bath-room, as have most of the Bedroom suites. Pure Water from Artesian Well. Finest and safest Otis Elevators.

General Manager, Mr. H. B. ROBARTS. *Hotel Manager*, Mr. K. SAILER.

SAVOY RESTAURANT

Of Gastronomic Fame. Dinners à la carte.
Private Rooms for Parties.

THE SAVOY DEJEUNER à prix fixe, 5/-, served on the Balcony overlooking the Gardens and River from 12 till 3. "THE OPERA SUPPER" 5/-.

The Orchestra plays during Dinner and Supper.

The Restaurant is under the direction of the famous Maître d' Hôtel, "JOSEPH," of the Restaurant Marivaux, Paris. Chef, Maître Thouraud.

PRIX FIXE DINNER (7/6) is served in the new Salle-à-Manger, on the Restaurant floor, at Separate Tables, from 6 to 8-30.

UNDER THE SAME DIRECTION AS THE SAVOY HOTEL.

The Grand Hotel, Rome.

The most beautiful and comfortable Hotel in Italy.

THE GRAND HOTEL RESTAURANT has been enlarged and redecorated for the present season. The cuisine equals that of the Savoy Hotel.

CHARMING SUITES OF ROOMS.

MANAGER - - - MR. A. PFYFFER.
(Proprietor of the Hôtel National, Lucerne.)

ALSO UNDER THE DIRECTION OF THE SAVOY HOTEL.

The Restaurant De Marivaux, Paris,

Known as "JOSEPH'S,"

VIS-À-VIS THE NEW OPERA COMIQUE.

A PERFECT CUISINE.

Maestro Boldi plays during Dinner and Supper.

CLARIDGE'S HOTEL,

Brook Street, Grosvenor Square, W.,

IN THE CENTRE OF FASHIONABLE LONDON.

THE "LAST WORD" IN MODERN HOTEL LUXURY.

Most beautiful suites of Rooms—all sizes—many of them specially suited for families who wish to avoid the trouble of a furnished mansion during the London Season.

ROYAL SUITE WITH PRIVATE ENTRANCE.

Single and double Bedrooms. Nearly one hundred Bath-rooms.

Manager - - - M. HENRI MENGE.
(Formerly of the Grand Hotel, Monte Carlo, the Hôtel Stahlbad, St. Moritz, and Proprietor of the Hôtel Bellevue, San Remo.)

Chef de cuisine - - - M. NIGNON.
(For three years head chef of Paillard's Restaurant at Paris.)

THE GRAND HOTEL
LIMITED
MONTE CARLO.

H. NOEL and PATTARD, Managing Directors.

OPEN FROM 1st DECEMBER FOR THE SEASON.

DIRECTORS:

Hon. A. BOURKE, of White's Club,
C. RITZ, } of the Hôtel Ritz, Place
L. ECHENARD, } Vendôme, Paris.

And also the Winter Righi at La Turbie.

See pages 127—133.

CAP MARTIN HOTEL

THE FASHIONABLE RESORT

Twenty-five minutes' drive from Monte Carlo

SPLENDID RESTAURANT

DÉJEUNERS AND DINNERS

A PRIX FIXE ET À LA CARTE

See page 58.

CIRO'S BAR

AND

HIGH-CLASS RESTAURANT,

GALERIE CHARLES III,

MONTE CARLO.

LUNCHEONS, DINNERS,
TEAS, SUPPERS,
'THE VERY BEST.'

See pages 43—49, 160.

Hotel and Restaurant de Paris,

MONTE CARLO

OPEN ALL THE YEAR ROUND.

The Nearest Hotel to the Casino.

L. DURETESTE,   Mons. FLEURY,
Proprietor.   Manager.

See pages 101—104, 163.

DAILY **The Riviera Times** DAILY

EDITORIAL AND PUBLISHING OFFICES: NICE

Published Daily during the Riviera Season
from 1st January to 30th April,
at **NICE** and the different **English Centres**
along the Coast of the Mediterranean,
from **HYERES** to **SAN REMO**;
and circulating throughout
Switzerland, Italy, Algiers, Cairo, etc.

Special Telegraphic and Telephonic Services from all the European Centres, supplied by Staff of Special Correspondents.

BEAULIEU-SUR-MER

THE
HOTEL BRISTOL

This Magnificent Hotel, specially built to suit English Requirements, and appointed in the most luxurious manner, will OPEN in JANUARY 1899.

HIGH-CLASS RESTAURANT.

FIVE MILES FROM MONTE CARLO.

See page 69.

HOTEL DES ANGLAIS
MONTE CARLO.

Entirely re-furnished and newly decorated by the new Proprietor.

PATRONIZED BY THE NOBILITY AND GENTRY.

Sanitary Arrangements perfect.

FINEST POSITION IN MONTE CARLO.

RESTAURANT AND TABLE D'HÔTE.

Ladies' Saloon and Smoking Room.

LIFT. ELECTRIC LIGHT.   *G. LUDWIG, Proprietor.*

WEINBERG & Co.,
43a, Duke Street, St. James', S.W.

Makers of the celebrated

"SPECIAL" CIGARETTES

as supplied to the Royal Family, London Clubs, and Regimental Messes.

PRICES: Large, 8s. per 100; Small, 7s. per 100.

Special terms for quantities.

Guaranteed of the very finest Yenidje and Mahala Tobaccos.

Particular attention is called to a new blend, mild and sweet, prepared especially for Ladies.

Plain, Gold, Aluminium, and Cork Tips.

GRAND HOTEL DU PRINCE DE GALLES

ET

GRAND HOTEL VICTORIA

MONTE CARLO

Specially recommended to Families.

Situated in the midst of large Garden. Elevated and climatic position. Superb view of Sea and Town. Apartments furnished with every regard for comfort.

350 Rooms. Conversation, Reading, Billiard, and Bath Rooms.

Lifts. Electric Light throughout.

Restaurant à la Carte and at Fixed Prices. Famous for good Cooking.

Proprietors, REY FRÈRES.

See page 163.

SAVOY HOTEL

MONTE CARLO

Facing the Casino, with View over the Gardens.

RESTAURANT

Déjeuners, fcs. 4; Dinners, fcs. 5.

CHOICE CELLAR. SUPPERS.

VOIRON, Proprietaire.

See page 164.

GRAND
Hotel St. James
MONTE CARLO

NEW FIRST-CLASS HOTEL, opposite the Casino and Public Gardens, offering every modern comfort, being the last built. Patronized by the nobility.

LIFT. ELECTRIC LIGHT.

SCHINDLER & Co., Proprietors.

See page 164.

HOTEL ROYAL
MONTE CARLO

ONE OF THE BEST SITUATIONS HIGH AND HEALTHY.

70 **Rooms and Saloons**, newly fitted up with modern convenience and comfort.

FIRST-CLASS FAMILY HOTEL.
OPEN ALL THE YEAR ROUND

CRETTAZ BROTHERS, Proprietors.

See page 164.

MONTE CARLO

Hotel and Restaurant
"PRINCESS"

Full South, overlooking Casino Gardens and Sea.

HIGH-CLASS RESTAURANT.

Luncheons, Dinners, and Suppers, Grill Room, American Drinks.

LOUIS AUBANEL, Proprietor.

See page 164.

MONTE CARLO

HOTEL WINDSOR
AND
HOTEL DE ROME
(ANNEXE).

Situated in the most charming and healthy part of Monte Carlo. Sanitary arrangements and Bath Rooms, executed by George Jennings, London. Arrangements may be made for a protracted stay.

LAWN TENNIS. LIFT.
ELECTRIC LIGHT IN EVERY ROOM.

A. GAILLARD and FAU, Proprietors.

See page 163.

HOTEL HELDER

MONTE CARLO

NEWLY BUILT.

FINELY SITUATED.

RENOWNED FOR GOOD COOKING.

See page 164.

===

Hotel and Restaurant de l'Europe

MONTE CARLO

Magnificent Terrace with view over the Sea.

ELECTRIC LIGHT.

Déjeuners fcs. 3; Dinners fcs. 4; including Red or White Wine

---

Special Terms for long Stay

FRANÇOIS RINJOUX, Prop.

Ex-Maître d'Hôtel of the

HÔTEL DE PARIS AND SAVOY HOTEL, LONDON.

See page 164.

Riviera Land Company,
LIMITED.

EZE-SUR-MER.

Situated on the high-road between Beaulieu and Monte Carlo.

A large Property has recently been acquired by an English Syndicate, who propose erecting an Hotel and Villas, and, generally, to develop the same on the most modern principles.

Eze-sur-Mer is most admirably situated at an easy distance from Beaulieu (2 miles) and Monte Carlo (5 miles), with both of which it is connected by an excellent carriage road and the railway, having a Station adjoining the property, through which more than eighty trains pass daily in the winter season.

Building Lots are now offered for sale on exceptionally advantageous terms.

It is proposed shortly to instal Gas and Electric works, together with a completed system of drainage. In a word, to transform this favoured spot into a Model Health Resort, replete with all modern requirements.

For full particulars, plans, etc., apply to

Messrs. SMITH & Co.,
Bankers and Estate Agents,
Galerie Charles III,
Monte Carlo.

NICE

First-Class Restaurant

THE LONDON HOUSE

See page 71.

NICE

Grand Hotel Terminus.

Opposite the Railway Station. Open all the year round. Latest Improvements, and Sanitary Arrangements perfect. Electric Light.

N.B.—Luggage is conveyed to and from the Hotel without any cost. Clerk to the Hotel takes Tickets and registers Travellers' Luggage. It is sufficient to leave the Hotel five minutes before the departure of the Train. Advantageous arrangements for protracted stay.

SPECIAL STORAGE FOR BICYCLES.

See page 143.

MISS S. E. BROWN,

COURT DRESSMAKER,

CHATHAM HOUSE,

13B, High Road, Knightsbridge,

LONDON.

Patronized by the Royal Family.

PATTERNS AND ESTIMATES SENT
TO ALL PARTS OF THE GLOBE.

BAGGAGE
TO AND FROM ENGLAND
PITT & SCOTT'S,
THE BEST AND SAFEST MEDIUM.

LONDON.
25, Cannon St., E.C.; 69, Shaftesbury Avenue; and Northumberland Avenue (adjoining Avenue Theatre).

LIVERPOOL.   **PARIS.**   **NEW YORK.**
4, Red Cross St.   7, Rue Scribe and 4, Rue Cambon.   39, Broadway.

CORRESPONDENTS

CANNES.—J. Valat, 9, Rue St. Nicholas.
NICE.—Scott & Co., 2, Place St. Etienne.
MENTONE.—Gustave Cochet, 1, Rue St. Michel.
MONTE CARLO.—V. F. Cursi, Ave de la Gare.

Hotel and Restaurant Dieudonné.

RYDER ST., ST. JAMES'S S.W.

Handsomely decorated in Louis XV. style.

Luncheon 3s. 6d.; Theatre Dinner 6s.; Special Dinner 8s.; Theatre Supper 4s. 6d. Service Special à la carte.

MANAGER, MR. AUGUSTE GIOVANNINI
(*From Grand Hotel Royal, Dieppe*).

PROPRIETOR, C. GUFFANTI.

Telegraphic Address, GUFFANTI, LONDON.
Telephone No. 5265, Gerrard.

PAQUIN

LONDON AND PARIS

Dresses

Mantles and Jackets

Tailor-made Garments

Rich Furs

Teagowns and Lingerie

Trousseaux

Each Design is Original, and produced simultaneously with its appearance in the Paris House.

PAQUIN Ltd.

39 DOVER STREET, MAYFAIR, LONDON

ST. MARCEAUX
CHAMPAGNE
(REIMS)

To be obtained at all the best Hotels and Restaurants throughout the World.

AGENTS:
PARIS, 18, Boulevard des Capucines.
LONDON, 5, Mark Lane, E.C.
NEW YORK, 21, South William Street.

See page 132.

A BOON TO TRAVELLERS
To and from the Riviera.

HENRY JOHNSON & SONS
LONDON, 39, Gt. Tower St., E.C., and Piccadilly Circus.
PARIS, 57, Rue d'Hauteville, and 2, Rue Scribe.

COSMOPOLITAN BAGGAGE EXPRESS
BETWEEN ALL PARTS.
FIXED INCLUSIVE RATES HOUSE TO HOUSE.
Insurance against Loss or Robbery in Transit.
Dry Storage at all depots 3d. per package per week.

BRANCHES—

NICE:	1, Rue Grimaldi.
CANNES:	3, Square Mérimée.
MENTON:	Rue Partouneaux.
MARSEILLES:	42, Rue Mont Grand.

List of Agencies, Rates, and fullest Information on Application.

HOTEL RITZ

RESTAURANT

PLACE VENDÔME

PARIS

OPEN SINCE THE 1st JUNE, 1898.

The appointments of this Hotel are unique in Europe. Every Room is fitted with a Private Bath Room, etc. Stylish Suites of Apartments.

The Restaurant with its extensive Terraces, lovely Gardens, and Fountains, is the smartest Rendezvous in Paris.

The Apartments overlook either the Place Vendôme or fine Private Gardens, and are exposed full South.

The Menton and Monte Carlo News
Should be read by every one

Contains the latest Society News
Lists of Arrivals
Programmes of all the coming Fêtes
Railway Time Table
Church Services, Cab Fares, etc.
Full reports of Fêtes, Parties

EVERY SATURDAY

Price, 20 centimes. Season Subscription, 5 francs.

Subscriptions and Advertisements received at—
The **OFFICES OF THE PAPER.**
SMITH'S BANK — Monte Carlo.
THE ENGLISH VICE-CONSULATE — Menton.

All Communications to be addressed to the Editor—
Rue Prato, MENTON.

KATE REILY

Court Dressmaker and Milliner

11 and 12, Dover Street, Piccadilly,

LONDON, W.

Sud de la France Railway Lines

1. Meyrargues to Nice (211 kilomètres) *viâ* Draguignan, Grasse and Colomars.
2. Nice to Puget-Théniers (59 km.) *viâ* Colomars.
3. Digne to St. André (44 km.).
4. Hyères to St. Raphaël (83 km.).
5. Cogolin to St. Tropez (10 km.).

☞ *The trains on the Sud de la France Line are in correspondence with those of the P. L. M. Co. at the stations of Meyrargues, Draguignan, Digne, St. Raphaël and Hyères.*

Tickets of the following kinds are issued:

1. At the principal stations of the line direct tickets (single or return) to the P. L. M. stations of Marseilles, Aix, Toulon, Nice, Cannes, etc. (and *vice versâ*).
2. Return tickets at reduced fares between all the stations and *haltes* of each line.
3. Excursion tickets at greatly reduced rates.
4. Circular tickets in connection with the P. L. M. railway for the following routes:

I.—Nice, Antibes, Cannes, Grasse, Le Loup, Colomars and Nice.

II.—Nice, Antibes, Cannes, St. Raphaël, Frejus, Draguignan, Grasse, Le Loup, Colomars and Nice.

III.—Nice, St. Raphaël, Ste. Maxime, Hyères, Toulon, Carnoules, St. Raphaël and Nice.

Buffets at the following stations—Meyrargues, Draguignan, Grasse, Colomars, La Tinée, Puget-Théniers and St. André.

Sud de la France Railway Lines
[*continued*].

For more detailed information apply to—

(*a*) The central administration at Paris—66, Rue de la Chaussée d'Antin.

(*b*) The chef de l'exploitation at Nice (Gare du Sud).

(*c*) The Inspector of the Exploitation of the Littoral line at St. Raphaël (Var).

Ask for Special Illustrated Guides to the Sud de la France Railway.

Principal points of Interest to the Tourist—

1. Between Nice and Grasse—Colomars (Manda Bridge across the Var), St. Jeannet, Vence, Tourrettes, the Gorges of the Loup (well worth a visit) and Grasse. Duration of railway between Nice and Grasse about 2 h. 20 m. Magnificent views all the way.

2. Between Nice and Puget-Théniers—Beyond Colomars, La Roquette-sur-Var, Levens, Gillette (lovely excursions); further on, Gorges of La Mescla and of Cians (very striking); the valley of the Vésubie; the village of Touët-de-Beuil (one of the quaintest to be met with, and a convenient starting-point for several excursions into the mountains); Puget-Théniers, and beyond that Entrevaux. (Time from Nice to Puget-Théniers about 3 hours.)

3. Between St. Raphaël and Hyères (coast line)—St. Raphaël and its environs, Valescure, Frejus (with its amphitheatre), Ste. Maxime (a little port and centre for beautiful excursions), St. Tropez.

NORTH GERMAN LLOYD,

OWNING THE LARGEST FLEET OF MODERN STEAMSHIPS.

REGULAR MAIL AND EXPRESS SERVICES
REACHING ALL POINTS OF THE GLOBE.

Bremen—Southampton—Cherbourg—New York.
Genoa—Naples—Gibraltar—New York.
Bremen—Galveston.
Bremen—Antwerp—Southampton—Genoa.
Genoa—Naples—Port Said.
India—China—Japan.
Java—New Guinea.
Genoa—Naples—Australia.
Bremen and Antwerp to South American Ports.

Among its largest and swiftest steamships are—

Kaiser Wilhelm der Grosse, Kaiser Friedrich, Kaiserin Maria Teresia, Kaiser Wilhelm II., Koenig Albert, Prins Heinrich, Prins Regent Luitpold, Barbarossa, Friedrich der Grosse, Bremen, Koenigin Luise, Lahn, Aller, etc. etc.

FOR PARTICULARS APPLY TO—

SMITH'S BANK,	**NORTH GERMAN LLOYD,**
Galerie Charles III,	2bis Rue Scribe,
MONTE CARLO.	**PARIS.**

www.ingramcontent.com/pod-product-compliance
Lightning Source LLC
Chambersburg PA
CBHW031830230426
43669CB00009B/1297